OXIDO DE MANCHAS
S SU ENEMIGO!
RUST SPOT
UR ENEMY!
你 的 敵 人 !

AUTH. F.P.C. 205.3635-DC

Dr. Ido's Journal

Alita is all that matters.

　　After Chiren and I were forced to leave Zalem with our ailing daughter, we rebuilt our lives as best we could. I will not lie and say that I do not miss our old life, but now I must view the last of the great Sky Cities from below.

　　Hanging suspended in the sky as if by magic (in reality, by engineering), I can understand the awe it inspires in so many down here on the surface, as well as the fear – there is something sinister about it, as well as beautiful. Perhaps that has something to do with the jagged hole torn in the center of the massive floating disk, where the debris and garbage of the privileged pour down into the Scrapyard beneath. Perhaps it is the fact that nobody from down here can ever go up. It's a rule that's never broken.

Just today, I was nearly crushed beneath an avalanche of scrap, when I got careless scavenging too close to a giant digging machine in the Scrapyard.

Iron City is a dangerous place, so I've decided to write this journal in the hopes that my work as a cybersurgeon will not be forgotten if I meet a violent end. Not for posthumous glory, but rather in the desire that someone will carry on what I have begun at the Clinic. And, most importantly, it is my deepest hope that this journal will inspire the reader to take care of Alita and her new body.

Most of my patients don't have the means to pay for my services, so I subsidize the Clinic with work tuning pro Motorball players, Paladins. The high speed, combative sport was created by the Factory to relieve tension here in Iron City. Because we come from Zalem, it was relatively easy for Chiren and me to find work as Tuners for the First League, the best of the best, making the huge cyber-gladiators faster wheel-feet, stronger armor, and more creative weapons.

I have a love-hate relationship with the violence and sheer spectacle of the game. Though Chiren seems able to view the "sport" far more dispassionately than me.

Today I worked on a relative newcomer who has been ascending quickly through the rankings: Jashugan. Cocky players all want to have "01" as their number so they can always say they're number one, but Jashugan took that a step further, choosing "00." Sure, his competitors joke how he's zero, he's nada, he's nothing, but he simply points out calmly that zero always comes first.

He came to me concerned about how much the grinding gears in his forearms were smoking during his last match. They just needed lubricating, but I wasn't going to argue when he called me a cyber-magician.

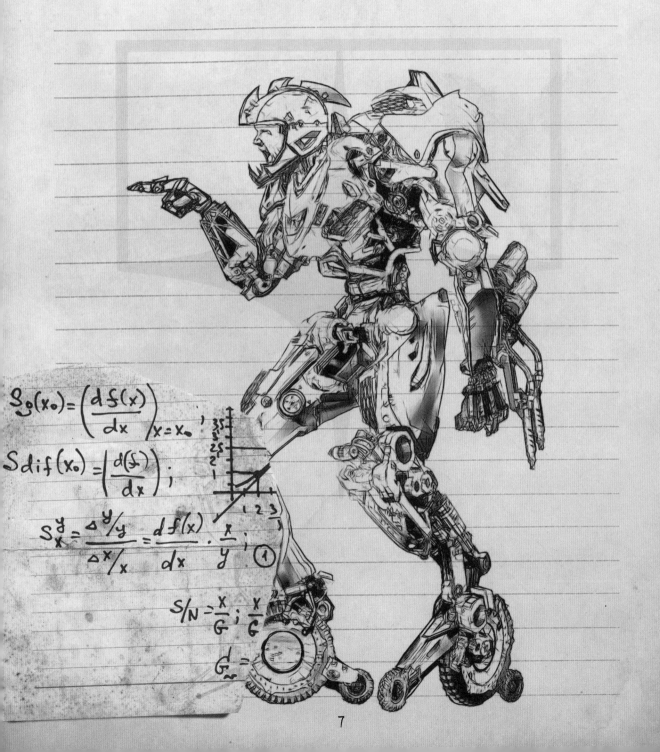

$$S_o(x_o) = \left(\frac{d f(x)}{dx}\right)_{x=x_o}$$

$$S dif(x_o) = \left(\frac{d(f)}{dx}\right);$$

$$S_x^y = \frac{\Delta^y/y}{\Delta^x/x} = \frac{d f(x)}{dx} \cdot \frac{x}{y}; \; \textcircled{1}$$

$$S/N = \frac{x}{G}; \; \frac{x}{G}$$

$$G \approx$$

FACT SHEET AND RULES OF THE GAME

TRACK DESIGN:

Track Architect – A. Todd Holland
Consultants – Steve Joyner, Ben Procter, Dylan Cole

TRACK SPECIFICATIONS:

Lap Distance – 9420 feet / 1.78 miles (2.87km)

Flat Center Width: 16 feet (4.88m)
Banked Surface Width: varies between 7 feet (2.13m) and 45 feet (13.7m)
Highest Banked Surface: 146 feet (44.5m) from ground level

Information correct at time of original construction, but now obsolete due to multiple renovations and additions in the years since.

Most of the track area utilizes a smooth concrete finish laid over a metal sub-structure. However, in high-bank curves, the top of the track is often replaced with a transparent Lexan barrier (to allow fans to see the action up close).

THE MOTORBALL – SPECIFICATIONS:

Diameter – 11.8 inches (30cm)
Weight – 88.2 pounds / 6.3 stone (40kg)

A combination of carbon fiber and steel skin surrounds various gyros and magnetics.
The ball is "motorized", making it move erratically during a match.

OFFICIALS:

(1) MOTORBALL CHANCELLOR:

The Chancellor has the authority over all League activities. His responsibilities include: broadcasting the games, hiring and oversight of referees, discipline of teams or employed individuals, and maintaining the Motorball track.

(2) GAME REFEREES:

Within the stadium, there are five (5) Game Referees, each with his own specific viewing station, from which he supervises one-fifth of the track. The Game Referees are audio-connected to the Chancellor, and their chief function is to call penalties and enforce the rules of the game.

(3) LEAGUE OFFICE:

Motorball's rules and regulations are maintained and updated by the Motorball League Office (MLO).

COMPETITIONS:

There are two styles of competition, TEAM and CUTTHROAT.

(1) TEAM

Two (2) teams of seven (7) to a side (First League Standard) generally play team matches.

However, teams of fewer than seven a side can often be seen in lower leagues as well as a three (3) team version, with five (5) players a side.

During a match, each team is allowed an unlimited number of substitutions, as long as there are not more than the initial allotments of players, which must also be listed on the game card prior to the beginning of the match.

Substitutions do not apply to players removed from the track for penalties.

(2) CUTTHROAT

Varies from five (5) to twelve (12) players, each playing individually (no teams).

Sometimes, larger variations of Cutthroat have been staged. The largest ever recorded Cutthroat match consisted of 45 players and lasted nearly two hours.

THE TEAMS:

STAFF:
Team Executive – 1
Team Tuner – 1
Mechanics – 3
Scavengers – 2
Motorball Players – varies per team.

(1) TEAM EXECUTIVE:
The general manager of a team, responsible for all the operations of the team on and off the track.

(2) TEAM TUNER:
The Tuner is responsible for the physical fitness and mechanical attributes of the team players, including research and development of new team equipment. *NB: Need to make sure I familiarise myself with any restrictions relating to the role*

(3) MECHANICS:
Mechanics are stationed in the Pit area and deal with mechanical malfunctions during a match. Those players seriously injured or no longer able to compete are taken away for medical attention or mechanical overhaul.

(4) SCAVENGERS:

Scavengers sweep the track of damaged equipment and, if required, injured players. They are considered 'off limits' to players; no deliberate contact is allowed.

(5) PLAYERS:

For a typical two team League Match, each team comprises seven (7) players, plus three (3) substitutes.

The substitutes are positioned in the Pit area during play until called into action.

UNIFORM AND EQUIPMENT:

1. Armor or pads are required; helmets are optional.
2. Propulsion systems* allowed.
3. No limit to number of wheels used.
4. Players must have "arms and legs". No pure wheeled vehicles or tank tracks allowed.
5. Weapons are allowed with the exception of projectiles**.

Review and approval from League Office required.

** *Projectiles include any type of gun, bows, spears, etc., or anything not primarily attached to a player. Flame-throwers are limited to six feet.*

BASIC RULES AND PENALTIES:

01. MATCH LENGTH

Two (2) Contests, each consisting of ten (10) laps.
(Note: variations are allowed if agreed upon by each team.)

After each Contest, there is a 20-minute break. If the score is tied after both Contests, an overtime Contest is played until a team scores, regardless of the number of laps.

02. START OF PLAY

The players line up at the starting line of the track. Once the motorball is launched on to the track, the players are free to begin play.

02a. Only one motorball is in play at a time.

03. PLAY

Any of the players on either team can field the ball and move forward as fast as possible to try for points.

A defensive player is allowed to intercept a ball being passed or pick up the ball that has been knocked out of the offensive ball carrier's possession and can immediately try to score points.

Penalties are enforced by sending the offending player (or players) off the track for a set amount of time to be determined by the referee. The player cannot be replaced during the penalty period.

O3A. The ball carrier is not allowed to deliberately hide the ball from the defensive team. The punishment for doing so is for the team to forfeit possession, called a 'Drop'.

During a Drop, no physical contact between teams is allowed. If there is contact, referees can levy a penalty.

Only a member of an opposing team can then pick up the motorball and play continues.

Note: A player on an opposing team is not required to pick up the motorball. However, if ALL the opposing teams' players pass the motorball without picking it up, the motorball is considered 'live' and any team can then take possession.

O3B. The players can only move in one direction (clockwise) around the track.

If a player is seen moving in the opposite direction (counter-clockwise) by the referee, a penalty is called against the offender.

STOPPING is allowed, but for no more than one lap by a teammate at any one instance.

O3C. At least two (2) players per team must be on the track at any one time (excluding Scavengers).

If a team fails to race (minimum) two (2) players, the match is considered a forfeit and the winning team given a 3-point margin of victory (used for League tables).

O3D. A player must not deliberately injure* another player. If he does so and is seen by the referee, a penalty is called against the offender.

* Only injuries to biological matter are of concern. Mechanical 'injuries' are part of the game.

O3E. The Scavenger personnel of each team are required to remove from the track as soon as possible injured players and damaged equipment.

If a player has deliberate contact with a Scavenger, a penalty is called against the offender.

O4. SCORING

O4A. In a typical ten-lap Contest, the team in possession of the motorball scores 1 point each time they pass a RED RING. There are three (3) Red Rings on the Motorball track.

O4B. A team gets a 2-point bonus if they manage to score all three Rings in a single lap.

O4C. Finally, the team in possession at the end of ten laps receives 5 points.

The Clinic was busy today and I struggled to cope, with Chiren out covering our Tuner work. I may have to see if we can find someone to train up as a cyber-nurse to help out.

The more Alita's health deteriorates, the more time Chiren spends away from home, from the Clinic. She denies the causal effect, arguing that she's not avoiding Alita, but rather working to save her. After all, if Jashugan's team wins the First League Championship, we'll get a bonus for our Motorball work that will allow us to finish the cyborg body we've been working on for Alita.

I like this one best. I wonder what Alita will think.

Chiren has a good point. While there's a part of me that's in no hurry to do a Total Replacement transfer of our little girl's brain, Alita will never get out of that wheelchair otherwise.

Alita told me today that she's really looking forward to waking up with legs that can run.

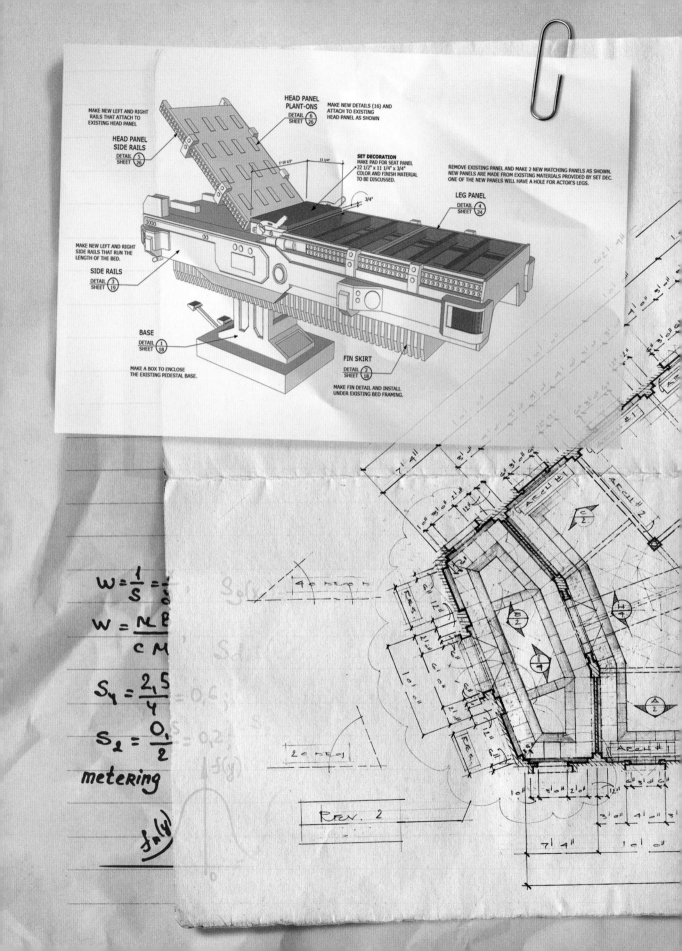

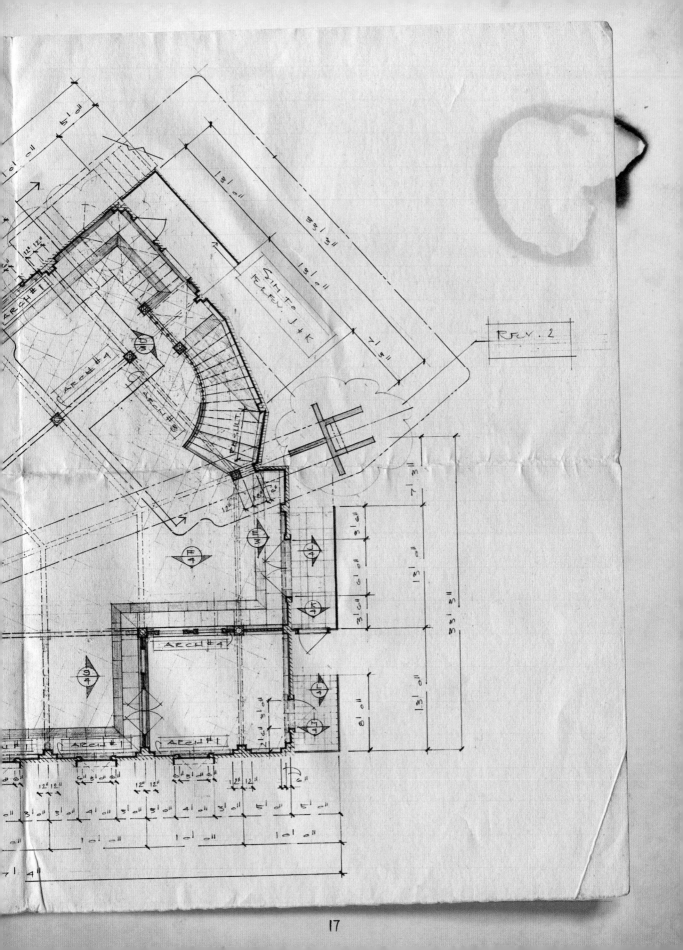

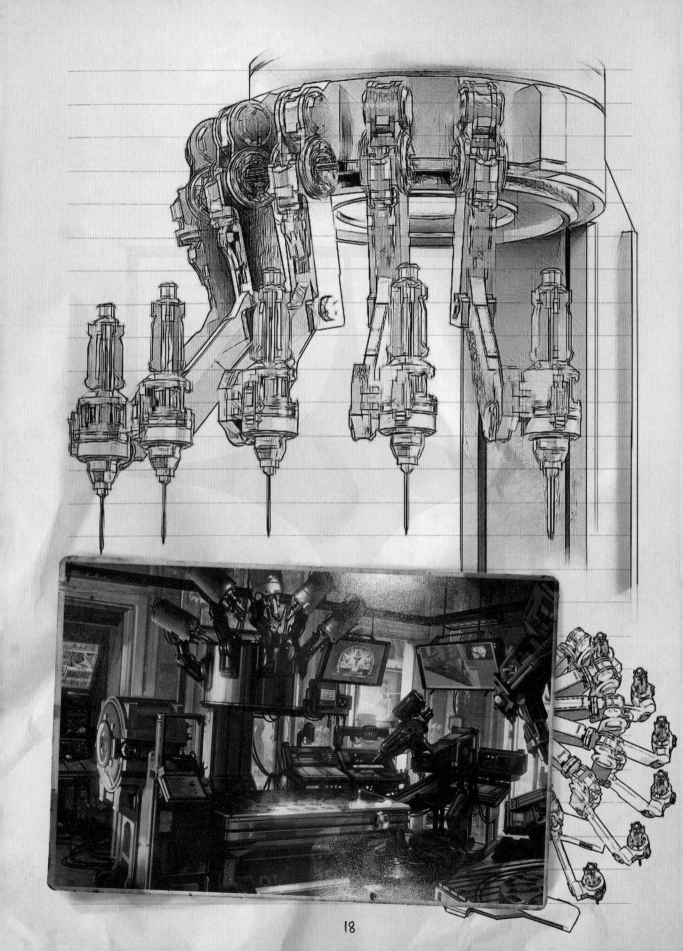

60.0

Today was one of Alita's good days. This morning she asked if she could add some more decoration to her wheelchair. She has a teenage girl's love for flowers and swirls, and would decorate all her possessions with them if she could. We came up with a design that incorporates the letter "A" that we could use for the back and wheels.

I suddenly realised that the body we've been building her is too plain. It doesn't reflect her vibrant, creative personality.

21

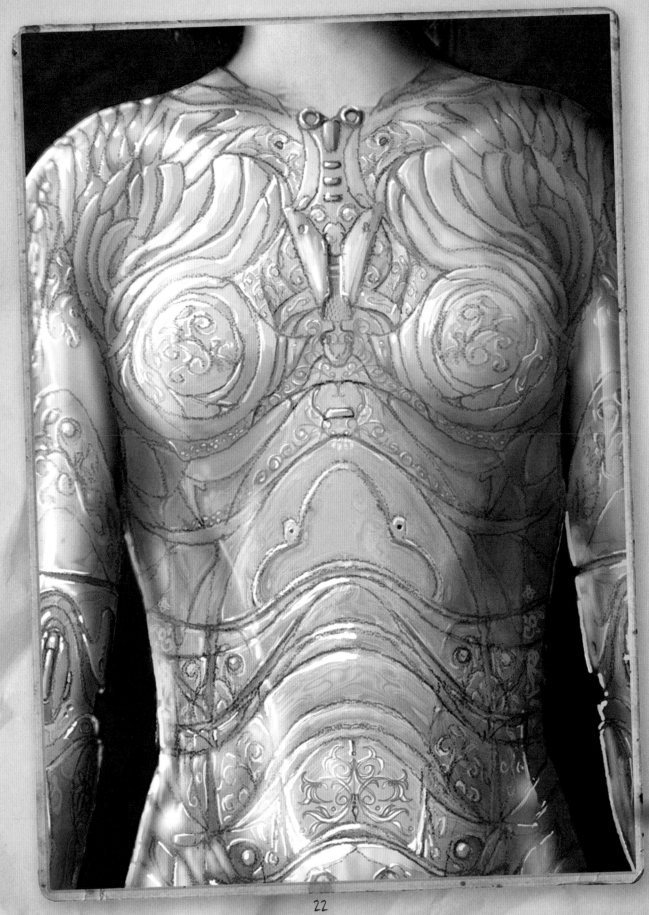

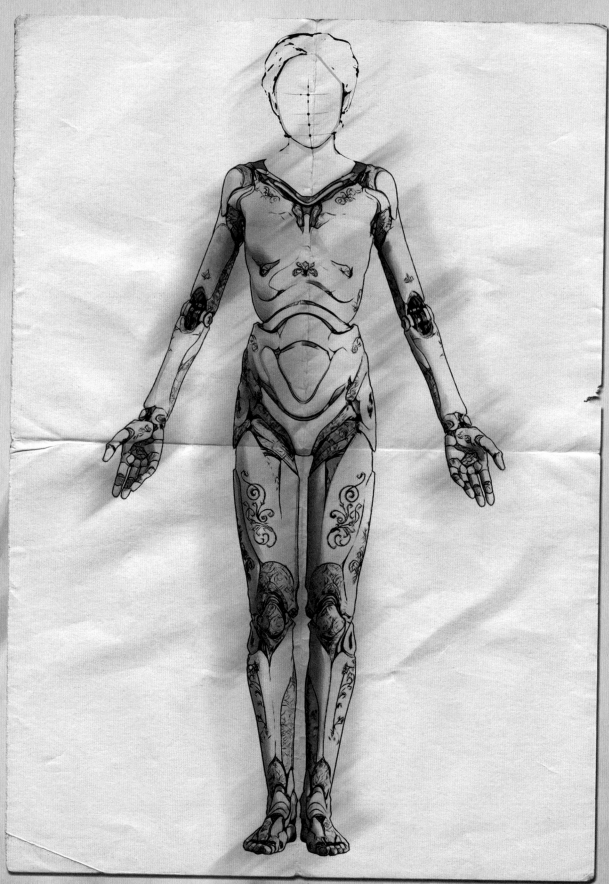

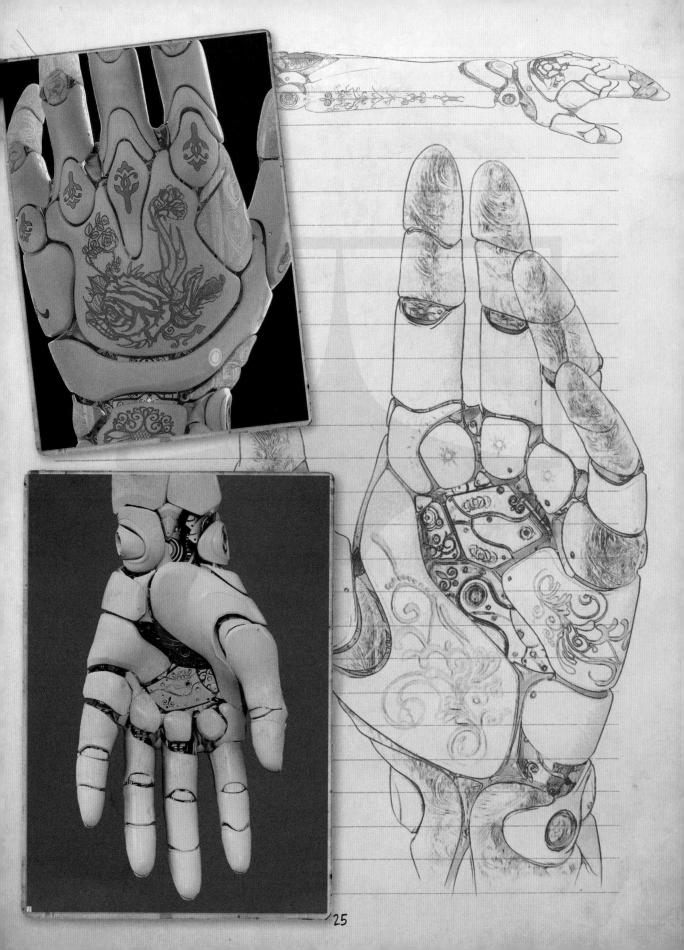

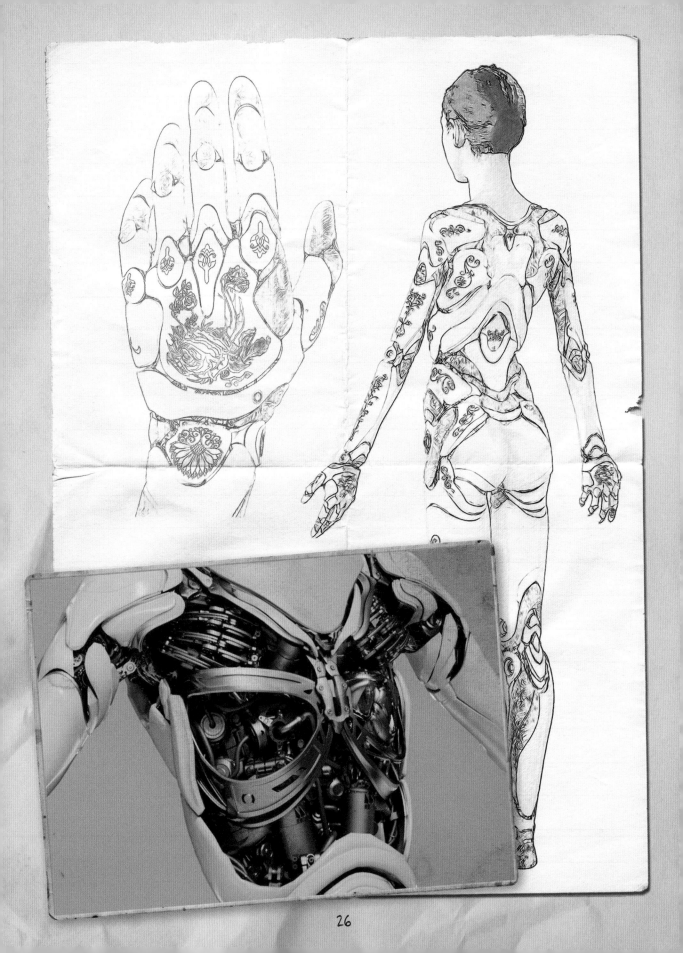

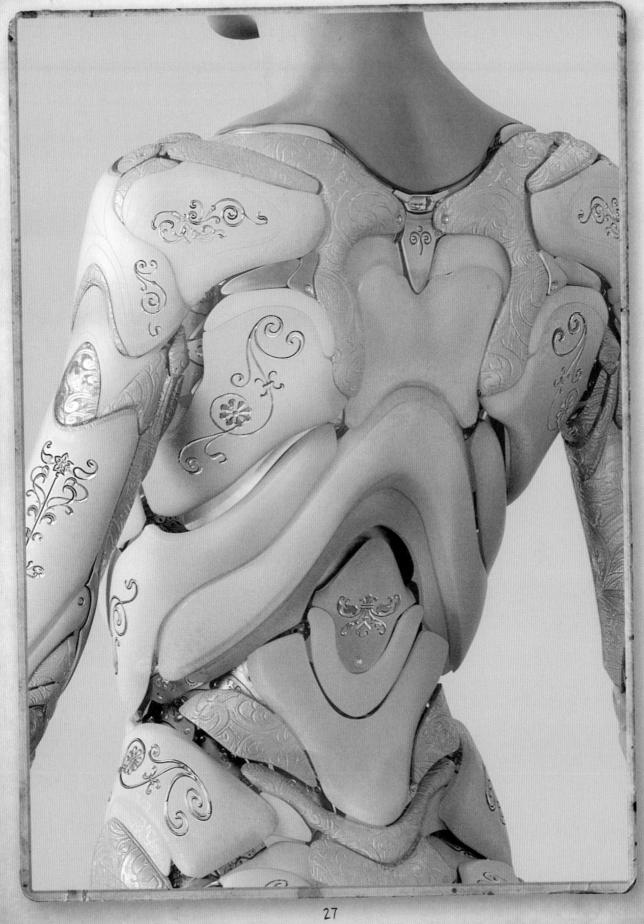

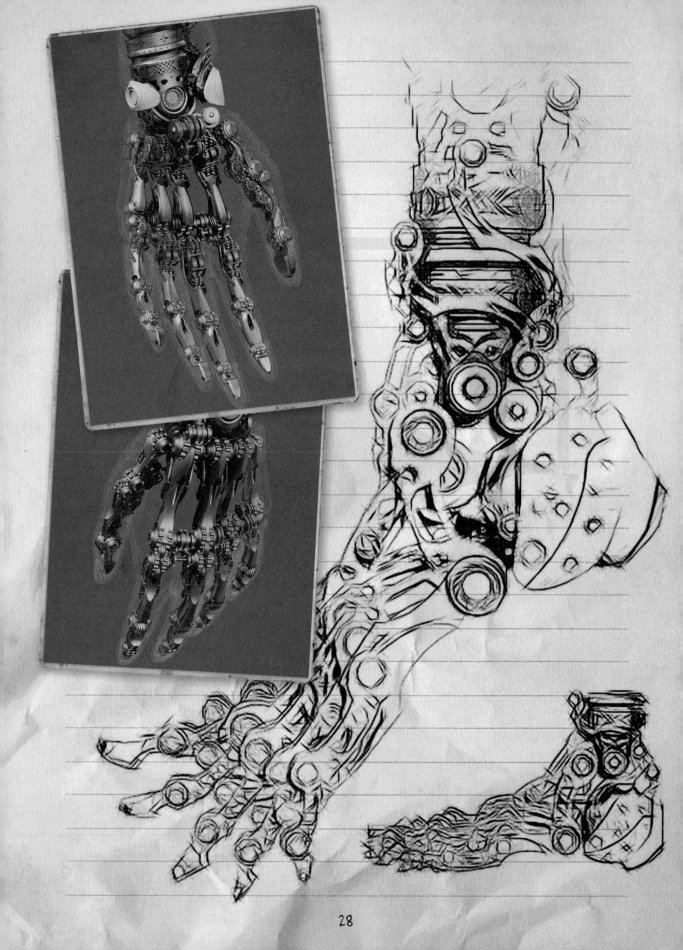

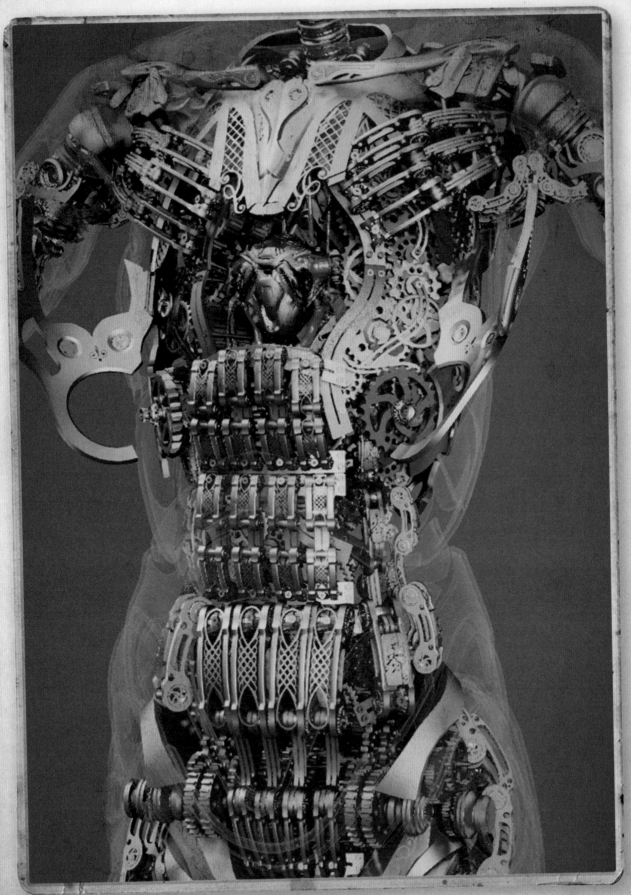

Jashugan won the First League Championship! I have to admit I wasn't expecting that. He was up against Grewishka and that beast was favored for Champion — I didn't think he'd let anything stand in his way.

For those born on the ground, the only way to get to Zalem is to become Final Champion by remaining unbeaten. There have only been a few since the sport was introduced, but I think Jashugan has the drive and focus to get there some day.

With the Grewishka upset, the media coverage exploded and Chiren got us into the spotlight. That secured our bonus, but it also brought our work to the attention of Vector.

Vector is a slick businessman who uses powerful cyborg muscle as his
bodyguards. He has ties to the Factory, and through that he's got his fingers into
all the main businesses of Iron City — legal and illegal. His influence is certainly
growing in Motorball. He approached Chiren and me with a too-good-to-be-true
offer to go work exclusively for him. Chiren seemed interested. I don't think she'll
ever give up hope of us returning to Zalem some day — she still wears the mark of
Zalem on her forehead. Vector doesn't sound interested in letting us keep the Clinic
going, though. That's a deal breaker for me. But even if he changes his mind about
that, for the time being I just want to keep the status quo and focus on Alita.
    Besides, I don't trust Vector.

I created a demon and he has sent me to Hell.

When he was a Paladin, I built him a machine body of obscene strength. Even then, I wondered if I'd gone too far… But before long even more powerful Motorballers came along and the game used him up and threw him away. He turned to drugs. Drugs he couldn't afford without his Motorball sponsors' funding. So he came to my Clinic to steal them…

He was obviously already blitzed out of his mind on something. He tore the lab apart, ripping cabinets off the wall. I tried to reason with him, to stop him, but he was beyond reason. My beautiful Alita, so close to being free of her wheelchair

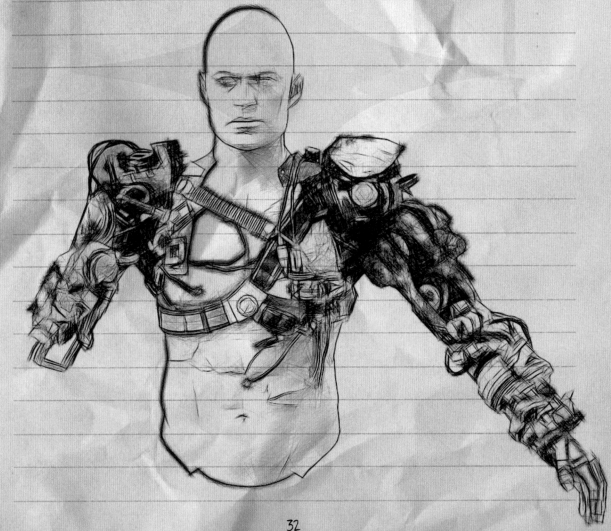

forever, couldn't get out of the rampaging cyborg's way fast enough. Her screams still echo in my ears as I write this.

Chiren can't look at me. She walked out of the Clinic without a word. I thought recording my feelings might somehow help me deal with my pain and hopelessness, but it's not working. I can feel my rage overwhelming me. And I know where to direct that rage...

I killed my demon.

I took a rocket-propelled hammer I had created as a prototype Paladin weapon and hunted him down. I needed to kill him, to obliterate him.

It brought me no peace. Killing Alita's murderer didn't bring my daughter back to me. Chiren is still gone. But I did find a new purpose. Part of me had wanted him to kill me, but I realize now that I'm not done hunting. There are other demons like him out there, and I'm responsible for all of them. We all are. So I registered as a Hunter-Warrior (#17739).

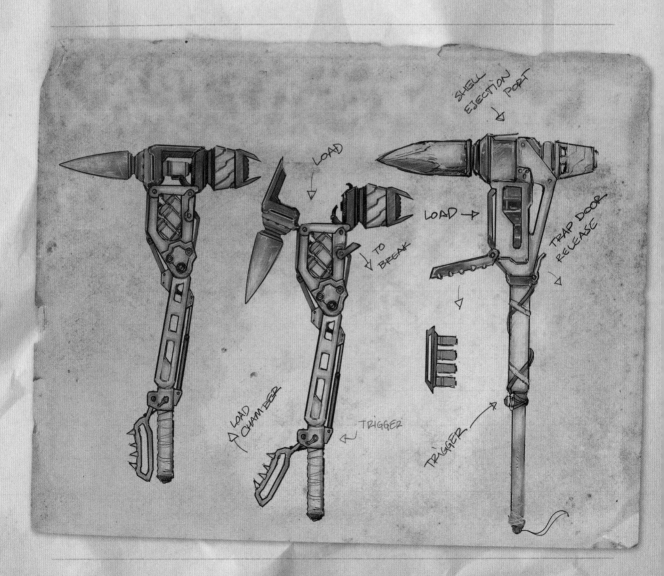

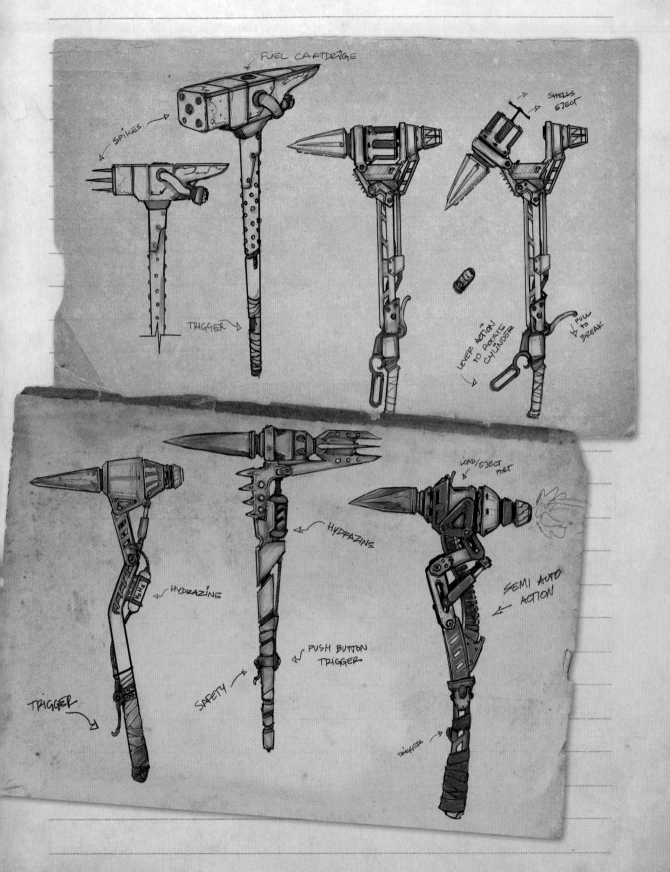

FUEL CARTRIDGE

SPIKES

TRIGGER

SHELLS EJECT

LEVER ACTION TO ROTATE CYLINDER

PULL TO BREAK

HYDRAZINE

HYDRAZINE

LOAD/EJECT PORT

SEMI AUTO ACTION

TRIGGER

SAFETY

PUSH BUTTON TRIGGER

TRIGGER

Last night I went to the Kansas Bar to let the other Hunter-Warriors know I'd joined the fold. Since there are credits involved, there's a level of competition, but the "heroes" of Iron City mostly share a rough camaraderie. And since I'd given a few of them free repairs at one time or another, my announcement was largely greeted with cheers.

Well, Master Clive Lee of the White Hot Palm didn't cheer – he's always very grim-faced, dressed in samurai armor, usually drinking alone – but he gave me a curt nod, which is practically a handshake from anyone else. Besides, with almost 50 confirmed kills in his first year as a Hunter-Warrior, he can afford to throw a few bounties my way.

McTeague, the "top dog", bought me a drink in celebration. I don't know who's fiercer, him or his cyborg-dogs. Yet none of them growled at me when I joined their table; even the canines were patients of mine, my scent familiar to them. Even still, I needed that drink to calm my nerves around those Hellhounds, having heard the stories about the bounties McTeague had failed to collect on account of his pets not leaving enough of the targets to identify afterward.

Screwhead bought me a drink, too. A screwdriver, of course. She was already tipsy, and she got a little touchy-feely, so I was grateful she just had two hands. In her street body, as a Hunter-Warrior, she has two arms, but when she plays Motorball for the Factory team, she has four. Her weapon of choice is a chain with multiple blades at the end. Rumour has it that she's shadier than most. I need to be careful around her.

Zapan turned the conversation to his favorite topic: Him. He's somehow gotten his hands on a weapon as flawless as his latest synth-skin face. He started referring to himself as "the Keeper of the Legendary Damascus Blade." Not that he knows any real legends about the sword or where it came from. Though from the glimpse I got while he was waving it around, it could be a genuine URM Berserker weapon, forged before the Fall. Its surface shimmers with an unusual iridescence, like a hybrid of metal and crystal. Honed to a monomolecular edge, it slices metal like butter. Which he demonstrated by slicing one of the bar's stools in half. The Barkeep was not happy.

I'd love to study it someday. If someone ever damages that precious face of his, I think I'll demand to examine the sword as payment for my repairs.

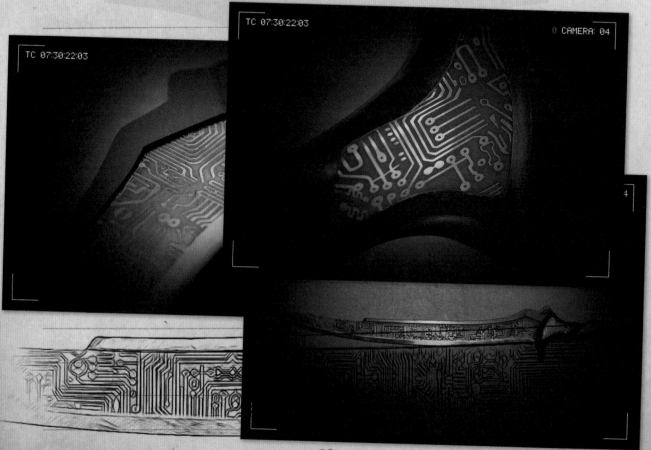

Hunted a criminal known as Sacredhorns, a partial cyborg with metal bullhorns. His poster is all over the Factory-run Bounty Kiosks scattered across Iron City.

He was living deep within the Scrapyard, in a veritable labyrinth of towering debris. I asked him why he didn't just call himself Cyber Minotaur, or Cybertaur, and he said, because when he attacks, the only way to survive is to bow down

before his sacred horns. It was good advice, as I simply had to duck under his head as he charged at me. Then I turned and swung my hammer and sent him to the seventh circle of Hell.

Claimed the Factory bounty on a pair of conjoined twins today. They weren't born that way. They chose to attach their heads to a single Total Replacement cyborg body so that they could always be together. Strange, but not criminal.

They crossed the line when they forcibly created themselves a two-headed boyfriend from a pair of brothers who most definitely did not want to share a cyborg body, especially since their human bodies had been perfectly healthy.

My rocket hammer split the ladies apart and I claimed two bounties for the effort of one.

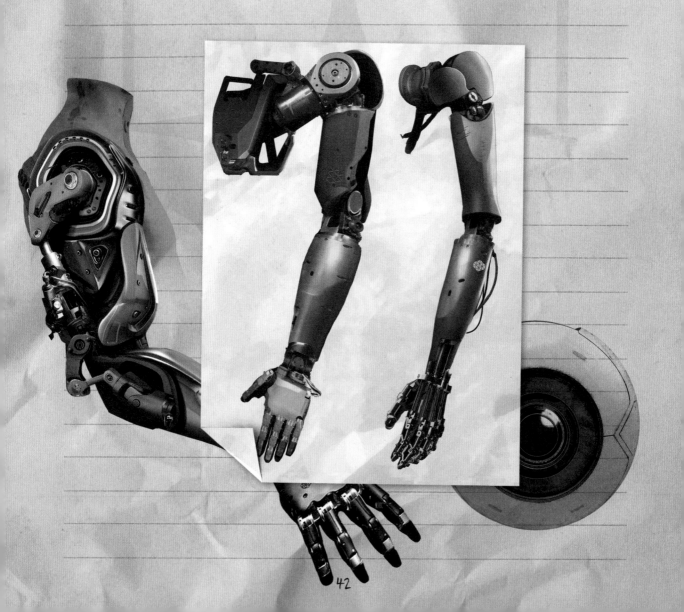

Alita is gone. No number of bounties will ever sate my need for vengeance.

Chiren is gone. Her way of dealing with the loss of Alita is to double her efforts to get back to Zalem. Of course, that's not possible. But she's turned to Vector and his empty promises. Deep inside she has to know he cannot give her what she desires, no matter how many Motorball Champions she builds for him. Even if she somehow does return to Zalem, it will not fill the Alita-sized hole in her heart. I can fix cyborg hearts, but I don't have the tools to fix my wife's.

I will never work as a Tuner again. I cannot work for a sport that creates monsters.

My hope is gone. I will continue my work in the Clinic, but I no longer see the purpose of this journal.

I have found something rare and precious. I have found hope.

I salvaged a cyber core unlike anything I've ever come across in Iron City. Such a remarkable discovery in the most unremarkable of places. I was scanning the Scrapyard for useable items for my Clinic patients and had thought I would find nothing better than a corroded steel hand and a glass eye saved from a burnt metal skull. But then I saw _her_, half-buried in a mound of trash. The angelic face of a young girl, her eyes closed, as if she was just sleeping.

I am not crazy. Though I nearly lost my will to live, I never lost my mind. I knew she wasn't my Alita, she wasn't my daughter. But as I looked upon this wrecked cyber core — barely more than head, spinal column, and heart, discarded like a child's doll that had been chewed by a stray dog — I knew that what she needed was the thing I'd tried so desperately to give my daughter: A new body. A new chance at life.

Her cyber-heart is still beating. Her organic brain is active. She is alive.

I brought her home.

TC 07:30:22:03

CAMERA: 04

Nurse Gerhad seemed shocked when I retrieved the cyber body I had made for Alita, but she didn't question my decision. She sensed my compulsion to save the cybergirl's life and helped me prepare the core for the transplant. I estimated the living human brain to be in the fourteen to eighteen year-old range, and was relieved when its machined skull fit the body I had made for a thirteen year-old.

Through it all, the cybergirl slept. As I watched her eyes move beneath their lids, I wondered what she was dreaming about. I wondered who she had been in her previous incarnation. Though I said nothing to Gerhad, I recognized the technology used in her cyber core. A precision-machined carbon-nanotube composite skull and a heart powered by an anti-matter micro-reactor. Lost technology from before the Fall. She is even more precious than I had first thought.

As her heart went from shuddering beats to a strong steady rhythm, with her red human blood pumping through transparent tubes and her iridescent blue cyber blood flowing through hydraulic and coolant lines, I saw a peace come over her face. She had been fighting to hold on to life... and she had won.

CENTRAL PARTICLE
ACCELERATOR MODULE

CYBER BLOOD SUPPLY
PERIPHERALS

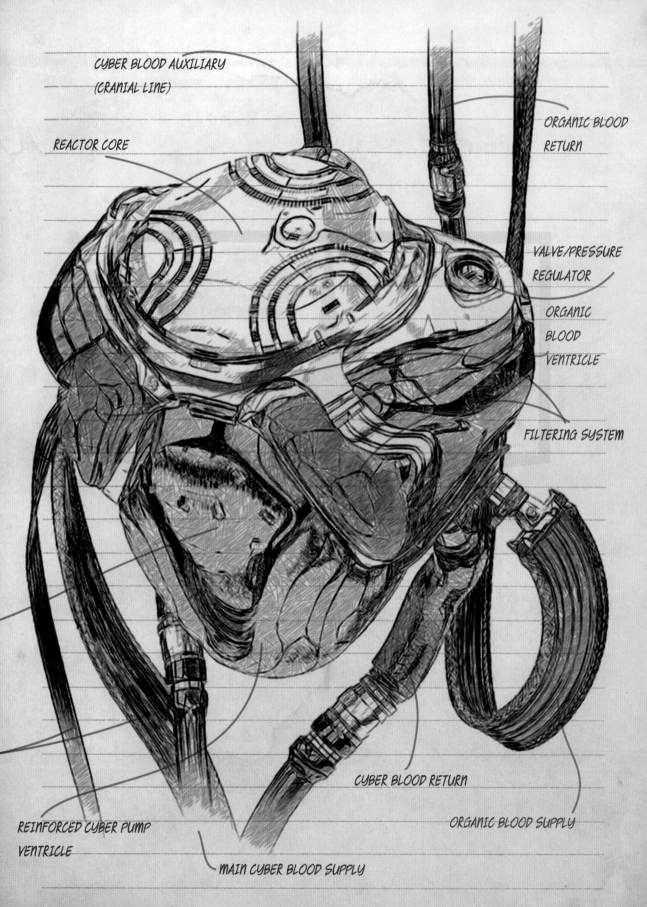

CYBER BLOOD AUXILIARY
(CRANIAL LINE)

REACTOR CORE

ORGANIC BLOOD
RETURN

VALVE/PRESSURE
REGULATOR

ORGANIC
BLOOD
VENTRICLE

FILTERING SYSTEM

CYBER BLOOD RETURN

REINFORCED CYBER PUMP
VENTRICLE

ORGANIC BLOOD SUPPLY

MAIN CYBER BLOOD SUPPLY

I used all my reserve credits putting the finishing touches on the girl's cyber body. Fortunately, I'd recently landed a profitable Hunter-Warrior bounty.

This one was a real nasty piece of work. A big ugly brute with steel fists the size of my head. He called himself "Double P," with the P's standing for Protector and Punisher. He ran an old-fashioned protection racket, demanding regular payments from local businesses in exchange for his protection from other criminals. He claimed he'd punish anyone who bothered his "clients," but the only people he ever punished were the clients who didn't pay him.

Double P had been on my radar for a while, but he was street savvy and despite his bulk, he knew how to disappear. Then he made the mistake of trying to shake me down. I've always tried to keep my Hunter-Warrior identity separate from my work at the Clinic, but when that thug came in there, threatening to tear the place apart if I didn't pay, I had flashbacks of the cyborg running amok through the Clinic.

I told him I'd get him a sack of credit chips and returned with my rocket hammer. I'm not too modest to say that I'm very skilled with that weapon, but none of my fights have ever been one-sided. This time, however, the bounty didn't stand a chance. He hadn't been expecting any challenge from me and he certainly hadn't been expecting the sheer rage that powered my first – and only – swing of the hammer.

While cleaning up the mess I'd made of Double P, Nurse Gerhad noticed something odd at the base of his skull. I scanned it and discovered a telepresence chip inside his brain. Somebody in Zalem had been riding him. I wasn't surprised. There are watchers-behind-the-eyes all over this city. Pretty common, now, unfortunately.

Double P's misjudged visit was well-timed for me in more ways than one: He was too early to see my latest Scrapyard recovery. I wouldn't want anyone looking too closely at my cybergirl, especially not someone from Zalem.

TC 07:30:22:03   0 CAMERA: 04

I have tweaked and fine-tuned every last circuit and connection on Alita's cyber body, yet she still has not opened her eyes. I'm beginning to worry. And Nurse Gerhad is becoming worried about me.

She has been a stalwart friend these past few years.

To take my mind off things, I went searching for an old model work arm, hoping to scavenge some spare parts, but I returned home empty handed.

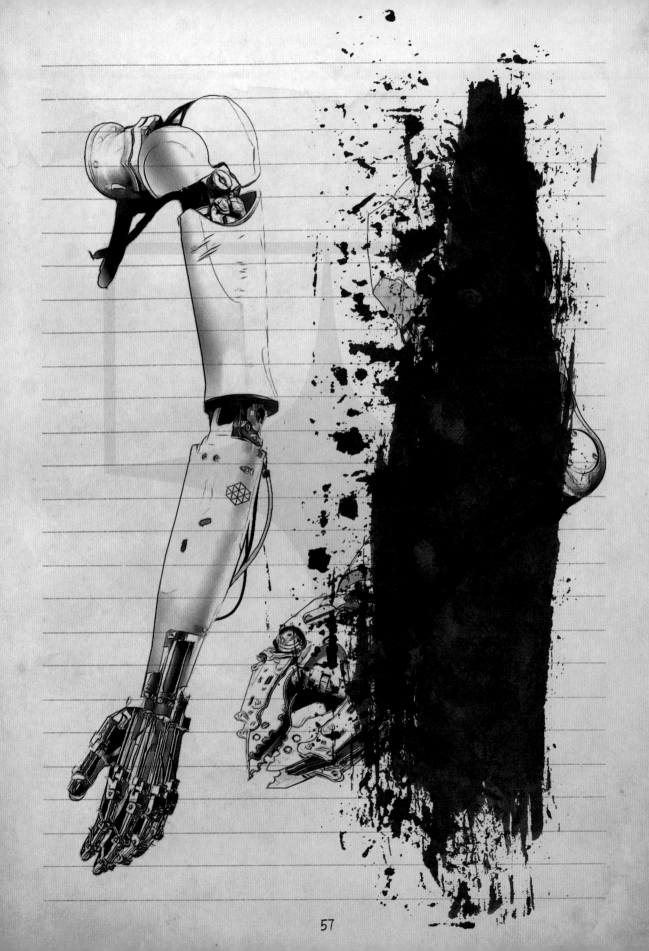

I broke the news to my patient that I couldn't find any used parts for his work arm. Even if the Factory worker could afford a new one – which he can't – they don't make his model anymore. His arm is massive and it keeps him employed, so he gladly settled for my repair work instead. The end-effector tools rotate smoothly now, so he was grateful. Paid me with a sack full of oranges that his wife got while working out at Farm 22. Nurse Gerhad would have preferred credit chips, but I didn't really mind; the oranges are delicious.

My next patient was a ghost. Cybergirl appeared out of nowhere, awake. Seeing her in Alita's body, in Alita's clothes, was like looking at a ghost.

I hid my awe and uncertainty behind a mask of professional curiosity. I calmed my rapidly beating heart and listened to her heartbeat: Strong and steady. I studied her eye movements. I examined her fully functioning cyber body.

With her up and moving for the first time, I am taken aback by how well her unique body suits her. It's not a run-of-the-mill metallic exoskeleton cyber body. I developed a unique creamy ivory synthetic skin, inlaid with silver flourishes and panels, which sits over a gold-plated skeletal frame. The panels are finely engraved with decorative scrollwork. She is truly a living work of art.

She was not experiencing any pain or discomfort, numbness, or motor dysfunction. She was, however, hungry. Thankfully, her taste receptors are working, so I gave her one of the fresh, sweet oranges to try. When she bit into it without peeling it, I knew something was off. It seems she's lost her memory. At the moment she is a blank slate.

I'd been hoping she'd give us some answers about where she came from. I told her that since she's a Total Replacement cyborg, and most of her cyber body had been destroyed, I couldn't find any records on her. Since her human brain was miraculously intact, theoretically she should remember something, so I'm at a loss to explain how her mind's so blank.

It was a lot for her to take in. In retrospect, I'm amazed at how well she handled the news. On the bright side, her tear ducts work fine.

I could barely contain my own tears when she later asked me to name her. With the body she's in, I couldn't help myself. I suggested Alita and she liked it. With the girl's loss of memory, it's like my beloved daughter has been given a new beginning. When she hugged me, I felt truly alive again for the first time in years.

We were both so excited by her rebirth – for want of a better term – that I just had to show Alita around Iron City. I need to keep in mind how dangerous the city can be for someone who doesn't even remember the necessity of staying out of the path of a honking gyrotruck. But I had to smile at how wide-eyed she was, taking it all in. She seemed particularly interested in the kids with wheel-feet and other TR cyborgs.

She noticed how the signs were in several different languages, so I explained to her about the survivors coming here from all over the world after the Fall. I thought learning about the war and about how everybody down here works for Zalem would bother her, but she took it all in stride. She just wanted to know if anyone ever goes to Zalem. The same question every child asks their parents sooner or later. Of course, nobody from down here can ever go up – Final Champions excepted. Despite Chiren's and so many others' dreams to the contrary, that rule is never broken.

It seemed like Alita was going to keep asking "Why?" endlessly, but then she got distracted by a four-story video screen on a nearby building, getting her first look at Motorball. I don't want her to waste her time watching that violent game, so I found her a better distraction – food. While Alita snacked on a falafel, I looked through some bins of rusted servos.

I had to squint to see some of the servo serial numbers, so I didn't notice her wandering off. But when I heard the massive Centurion mobile gun platforms marching down the street, I made sure she knew to stay out of the Factory enforcers' way. I found her with Hugo, a young man who supplies me with parts of sometimes-dubious origin. He made a joke about Alita diving through the Centurions' legs. I was not amused. Her body was not created for confrontation.

Alita seems quite taken with Hugo. Though I am wary of the reasons for his apparent interest in her.

I hope his recklessness doesn't rub off on her. Still, for growing up in a desperate place like Iron City, he's a good kid at heart. And he got me the driver boards I was looking for. He's certainly resourceful.

Now that I have Alita in my life, I have to be more careful. Last night I injured my forearm fighting a bounty. I threw up my arm just in time to block a blow to my head. I almost died. I can't leave her alone. Not when we just found each other.

I'm still concerned that Alita wants to hang out with Hugo and his friends. Some of the parts he's gotten me were definitely jacked. I'm not saying he's a jacker, but he has dealings with them at the very least, so being around him is not exactly a safe place for a TR like Alita.

Take that poor patient I got in today. His buddies brought him in after he had his arms and legs stolen. He said the jackers ripped him to shreds right in front of a Centurion. The Factory looks the other way because they want the jacked parts on the black market to supply Motorball. It's despicable.

I wish Alita didn't have to see things like that, but I guess it's best that she learns how dangerous this place she woke up into can be.

Nurse Gerhad is training Alita to assist me, so she'll be seeing a lot more jacker victims. Alita's a really fast learner. Maybe, if something does happen to me, they will be able to keep the Clinic going.

I know I said I have to be more careful, but there's an unidentified large cyborg murdering young women and I won't sleep until I know Alita's safe. The wanted poster has the death count at six and the bounty at 10,000 Factory credits. That's a low reward if you ask me, especially if what my patient said is true, that the murderer carves up the women and puts them in little metal boxes.

I made Alita promise not to go out after dark for now, but she's a teenage girl, so we'll see how long she'll hold to that...

Chiren saw Alita today. I guess it was inevitable. I tried to pass her off as my new assistant, but Chiren recognized our daughter's cyber body. Chiren wanted me to destroy it years ago, remove one of the biggest reminders of our loss. I hadn't wanted to argue with her, so I agreed, but I never had any intention of destroying it. I couldn't.

Chiren handled the encounter better than I thought she would. Maybe she really has managed to move on. She says now she wants me to move on, as well. That it's time for me to stop being noble. I've done my penance for creating our daughter's murderer. She tried to lure me away with the promise of brand-new equipment... and of us being a team again. I'm no fool, I know she's with Vector now, but the way she looked at me, I could almost convince myself she still loved me.

More than anything, she wants to get back to Zalem. But she's not entirely self-centered. She seemed sincerely to want me to go with her. I'm needed here, now more than ever, but if I knew a way to get her back to Zalem, I would help her in a heartbeat. Only, there is no way back. She thinks Vector and his "high connections" will get her there. She's that desperate.

69

    She pointed out the Paladin Claymore. Said
he's one of her creations. He's pretty fierce. Looks
like a medieval knight, with a mace that could
take out a Centurion.

    I would still do almost anything for Chiren, but
I can't help her build Motorball Champions. They
have a nasty way of becoming killers. They wind
up back on the street, junkies with big hydraulic
arms and bad attitudes. She seems to have
forgotten that.

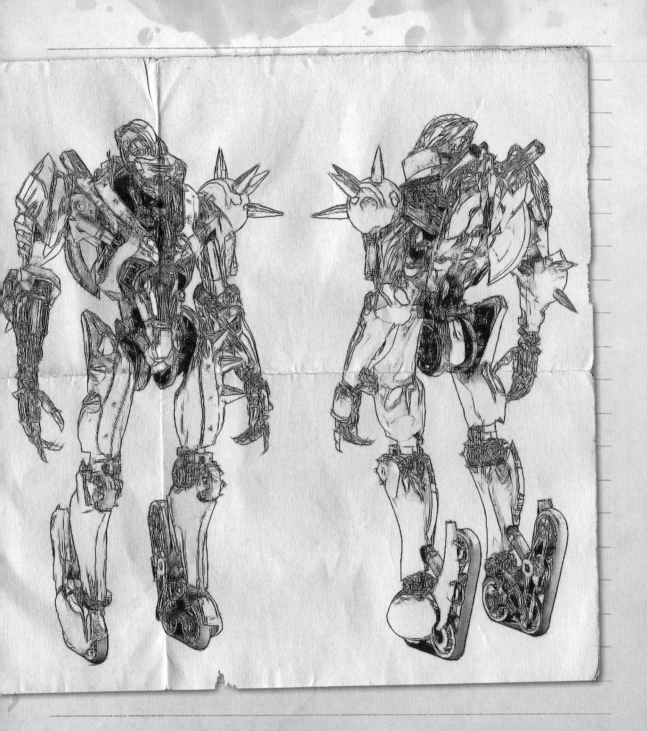

Alita apparently forgot how to keep track of time, coming home after dark. I'm sure she was with Hugo. I warned her not to trust anyone. People can do terrible things to each other here. But Hugo introduced her to chocolate, so now she probably thinks he can do no wrong.

Alita saved my life last night. I should be angry with her for breaking her promise to stay in at night — not to mention thinking I was murdering women! — but I'm glad she did.

I was keeping an eye on a woman walking alone after dark, as she fit the killer's victim profile to a tee. Indeed, she led me right to him! And his partner. But she was a perpetrator, not a victim. She was working with them, too. I walked right into a trap... and Alita followed me.

I took on Romo first. He seemed to have a liking for blades, with a scythe-like knife attachment in place of his left hand and wielding a miniature scythe with his right, but I tore his forearm clean off with my hammer. My next swing missed its mark and he slashed my shoulder, knocking my hammer away.

Before I could get my weapon back, the fake damsel in distress stepped in front of me and put a long blade to my throat. A blade that turned out to be a metallic praying mantis-like forearm. I recognized this bounty: Nyssiana, a TR cyborg with a liking for insects. And an unhealthy interest in my eyeballs.

TC 07:30:22:03   0 CAMERA: 04

    With the first cloaked hulking brute standing in the shadows, I was surrounded by three powerful cyborgs, my weapon just out of reach. I knew I was done for, but I couldn't bear to see Alita die. Again. I shouted at her to run for her life.

    She ran all right, but not to safety; she ran toward the fight. Slamming into Romo and then proceeded to punch him so fast and hard that within seconds there was nothing left but a junked pile of scrap.

    Unsurpisingly, that enraged the hulking criminal, the one wanted for the murders of all those women. He actually roared in anger as he threw off his cloak and showed his face. I recognised him — another Motorball Paladin turned killer. Grewishka. He ordered Nyssiana to rip Alita apart.

    I got my rocket hammer back, thinking I could attack Grewishka while he was focused on Alita, but he saw me coming and grabbed the hammer with one enormous hand. He pinned me to the wall and forced me to watch the fight. Nyssiana was all wild slashes, in contrast to Alita's graceful movements. Then, in a blur of motion, Alita jumped up, her tiny body generating a shattering force as she drove Nyssiana's cyborg head into the wall, crushing the metal skull.

Seeing his companions die didn't scare Grewishia off any more than he scared Alita. She charged right at him, then leapt over his swinging hydraulically powered arm. But as

amazing as her fighting skills were, she underestimated her opponent. Years in the Motorball arena had given him lightning reflexes. Grewishka was ready for the move and backhanded her, knocking her half-senseless toward a wall. Yet somehow, she snapped out of her daze at the last second, performed a seemingly impossible midair spin and landed on a section of wall.

I distracted Grewishka so Alita could catch her breath, but she didn't waste the opportunity resting. As the monster was knocking me on my ass, she hurtled down toward Grewishka with a fierce war cry that seemed out of place coming from her small mouth. She drove her feet into his shoulder, the impact shearing his arm right off. She found my rocket hammer and smashed it into Grewishka's chest, shattering his armor.

I could only watch, stunned, as Alita hefted the hammer and strode toward Grewishka, who staggered backward in pain. She swung the hammer at his head, but he avoided it and vanished into the darkness. He left us with the chilling parting words: "You'll pay, little flea... Grewishka does not forget! I'll be coming for you both."

Alita looked ready to chase after him. I was disturbed by her intensity, and unnerved by her fighting skills. Seeing her moves triggered the hint of a memory in me. Of something I saw once in Zalem. In my former life. Something I'm not sure I want to remember.

She killed two of the most notorious criminals in the city, and pissed off a third. Grewishka will come for us, of that I have not doubt.

I explained to Alita how before the Fall there were police to stop criminals. Now the Factory just licenses Hunter-Warriors to do the dirty work and pays them bounties. Since Alita doesn't have an I.D. badge, Hunter-Warrior 17739 got credit for the kills. The price on Nyssiana's head — literally; the Factory Deckman scans the head to authorise payment — was twenty thousand credits. The bounty for Romo was fourteen thousand credits. Thirty-four thousand is a good haul, but I wasn't thinking about the money. I was more concerned with the hurt in Alita's voice. It didn't matter to her that the money kept the Clinic open. She wasn't bothered by my being a Hunter-Warrior, just by my keeping it a secret from her.

I didn't want to tell her why I started hunting. Not her of all people. But she's starting to remember her past and I owed her an explanation. So I told her about my daughter. I took her home and showed her a holo photo of my daughter taken during those last days. I told her everything from how I'd been a Tuner for the First League to how I'd become a Hunter-Warrior.

She asked if I'd ever found peace. That's a hard question to answer. If I'd reflected on it, I probably would have said no, because there isn't a day goes by that I don't rage at the universe over the death of my daughter and the end of my marriage. And I really can't see myself ever truly coming to terms with the fact that I will never see my daughter grow up into a woman. But I still answered honestly when I told her that finding her gave me peace.

I was relieved my examination revealed no internal damage inside Alita's cyber body. She walked away from that violent encounter with just some cracked bushings in her leg. Still, I hope she does take things easy until I get them replaced. Although it seems she's wired for pretty much the opposite of taking things easy.

I would have preferred Alita had the chance to develop like a regular teenage girl, but I couldn't hide the truth from her any longer. I showed her my scans of her cyber core, especially her heart. Its tiny micro-reactor could power all of Iron City for years.

It was difficult to break it to Alita, who we've all treated like a teenager, that her pre-Fall technology means she's actually over three hundred years old.

Alita told me she had flashbacks during the fight with Grewishka's gang. She was on the moon wearing battle armor and attacking a squad of enemy cyborg soldiers. Warships engaged in a fierce battle overhead as she killed the soldiers ruthlessly and without hesitation.

Somehow, Alita must have entered a time field which placed her in suspended animation to enable her to have survived centuries. That may also explain her memory loss.

Now more than ever I am convinced that in her previous life she was someone very special, and very important. But I need one piece of tangible evidence before I can bring myself to tell her everything I believe she is capable of.

It worries me that there's no bounty on Grewishka. I gave a full report of my encounter with him — minus a few minor details about Alita's involvement. I left no room for doubt about him being the one who'd killed all those women, yet even his old criminal bounty had disappeared. I briefly allowed myself to imagine he'd died after battling Alita, and someone had found him and collected the bounty on him, but no, there is no record of his death. The only explanation is that somebody's protecting him. Somebody far beyond us here.

The wise thing to do would be to stay off the streets for now. Impulsive teenagers don't always make the wisest decisions. Alita says she wants to become a Hunter-Warrior. She wants us to be a team. How could I ever focus on hunting if I'm always worried about leading her into danger? She says I'm holding her back. In a way, I guess I am. For good reason. Her body's not built to take that kind of combat stress.

I could make her body stronger, tune her like a Motorball champion, but I don't want blood on those hands. I built her hands to create, not destroy. Alita doesn't see it that way. For her, combat is a way to remember who she was, to feel who she was. What she doesn't seem to understand is that some things are better left forgotten.

Things like Berserkers.

Alita was an URM Berserker. She ran off with Hugo today and he took her to the Badlands, to the site of a crashed URM warship. She gained entry and found a Berserker body inside. She says she has a connection to it she can't explain. It was almost as if it called to her. It is sleek and powerful. It will give her the strength she needs to survive if she insists on becoming a Hunter-Warrior... which is why I refused to put her into it.

Of course, even if she doesn't actively go after bounties, that doesn't mean she won't wind up fighting Grewishka and anyone else he sends after us, so I'm conflicted. Still, she's been given a chance to start over with a clean slate. How many of us get that chance? She doesn't need to be a warrior, she can be something safer.

Alas, she has the temper of a born warrior. The dented metal table in the Clinic will be a constant reminder of that. So I told her the truth about where she came from. Her core was designed to interface with a Berserker body, which is a humanoid weapon-system created by the URM Technarchy. The identity code in her temple activated it.

I also told her how her instinctive fighting technique is a lost combat art for cyborgs called Panzer Kunst that was used by the Berserkers. Panzer Kunst was the deadliest fighting style in the galaxy. Only fragmentary records of its practice remain. That's why she's drawn to conflict without hesitation. It's part of her training.

Alita is not just a warrior, she's the most advanced cyborg weapon ever created. And that is why I will never unite her with that Berserker body!

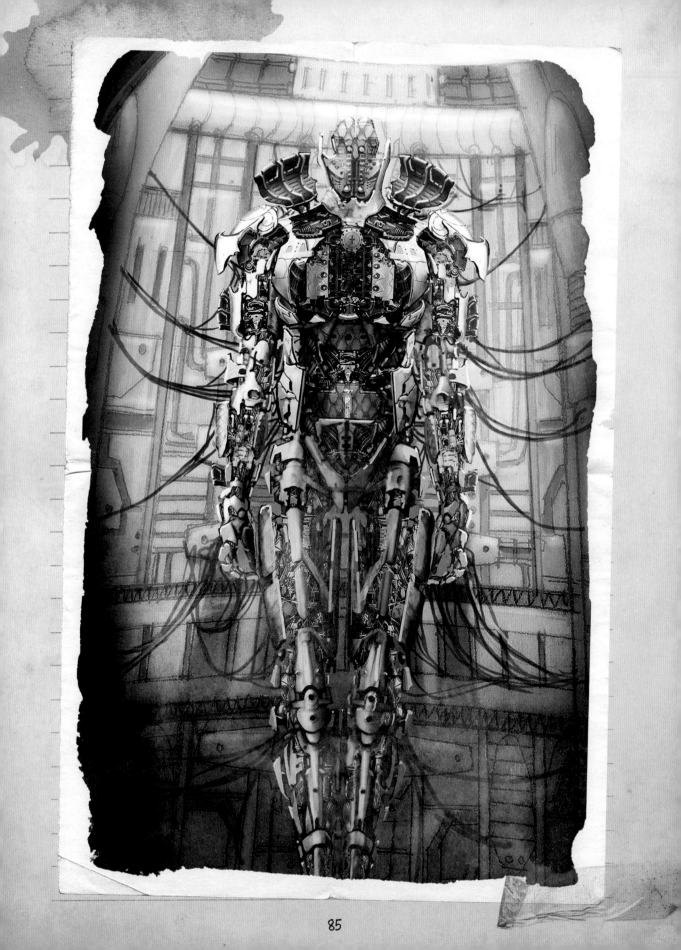

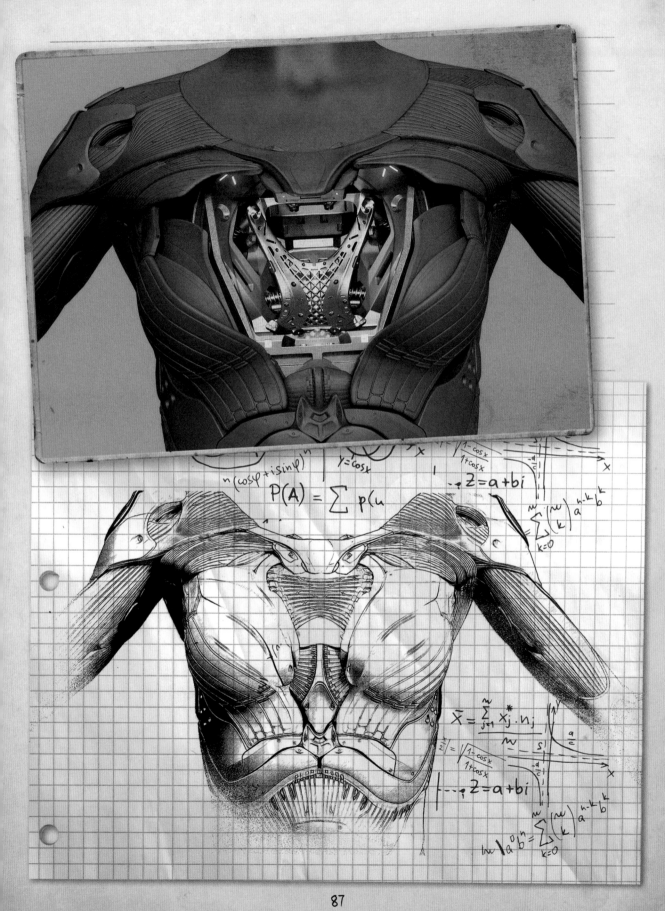

$$P(A) = \sum p(u$$

$$\bar{X} = \frac{\sum_{j=1}^{n} x_j \cdot n_j}{n}$$

$$z = a + bi$$

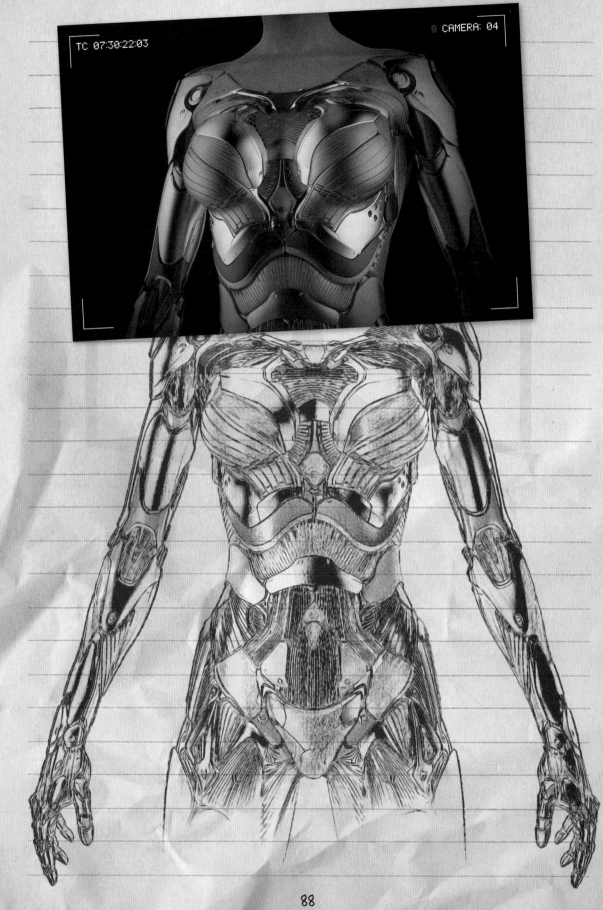

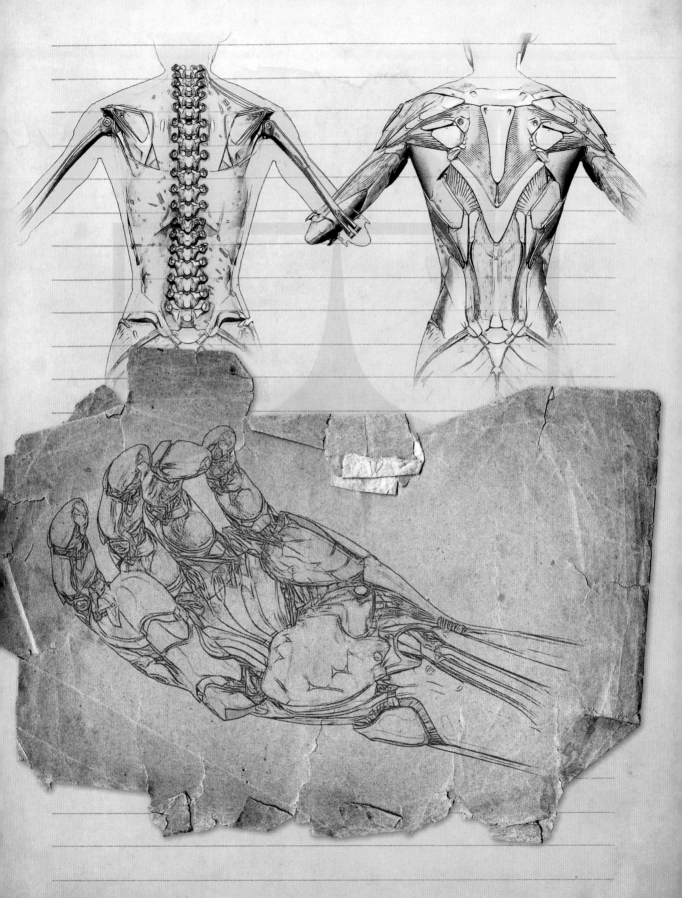

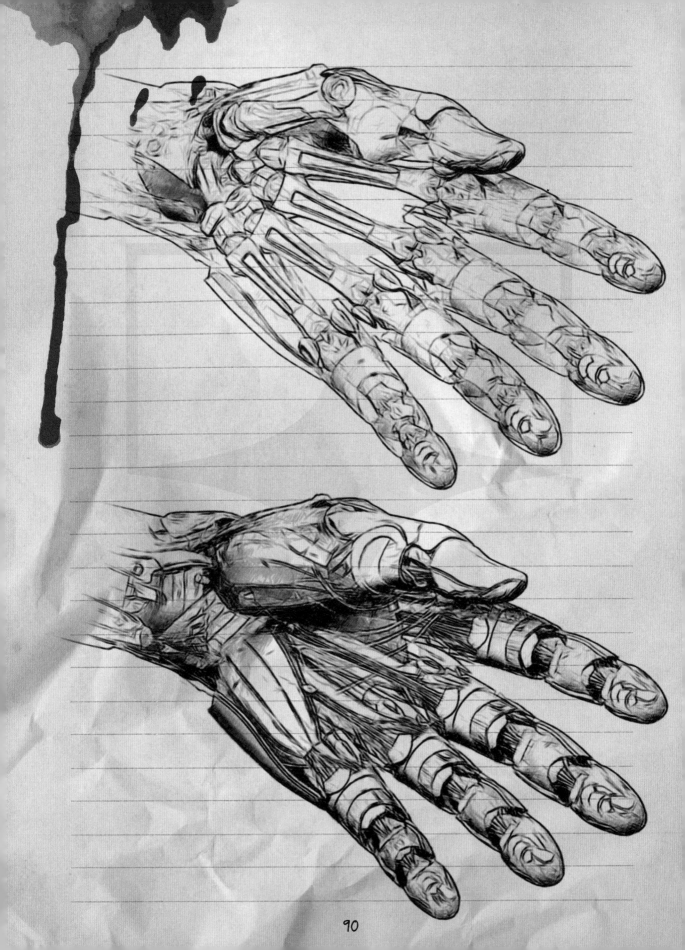

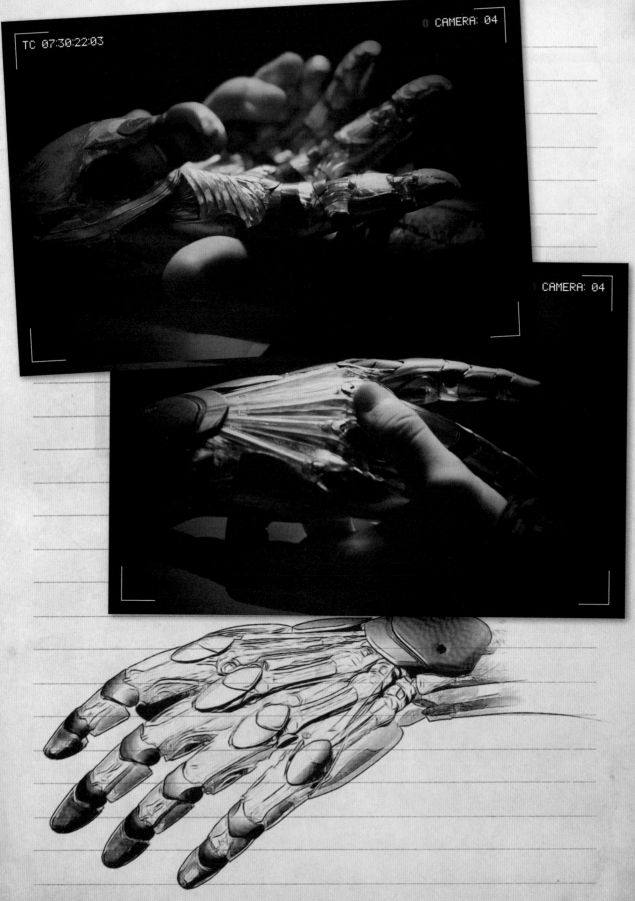

I had a feeling Alita would not back down from becoming a Hunter-Warrior. She's a typical rebellious teenager in that sense. But I didn't expect to find her at the Kansas Bar last night, in the middle of a barroom brawl — which she started!

Though it seemed Hugo had her back, at least. When I walked in, I saw a Hunter-Warrior swinging a chair at Alita and I knew I was too far away to stop it. Hugo leapt in, quick as a ferret, and zapped him with his paralyzer bolt.

Then I was able to break things up, pushing people apart with my rocket hammer. I made it very clear that anyone who kept fighting would forfeit my goodwill, meaning no more free repairs. That sobered them up.

Alita stood in the middle of the room while the hunters she'd knocked down staggered to their feet. I tried to take her aside to talk some sense into her, but she blamed me for her behavior, said I hadn't left her any other choice. Then, before I could give her many other choices on how to live her life safely, Grewishka burst into the bar. Literally: He smashed apart the transom on his way in.

That cyber ape was huge before, but he'd been repaired impressively. No, not repaired, remade. His body is massive, his arms twice as thick as before and longer, apelike. I'm sure I recognized some of Kinuba's jacked armor on him, and Grewishka's right hand sported grind-cutter razor-edged fingers.

A Hunter-Warrior I didn't know too well made the mistake of asking what had happened to Grewishka. That got the thug's attention and without a moment's hesitation, without any humanity whatsoever, he shot out one of his bladed "fingers." The high-velocity cutter slashed back and forth through the Hunter-Warrior in the blink of an eye... and then reeled back into Grewishka's hand, snapping back in place at the knuckle. There was stunned silence in the room as his victim fell to pieces.

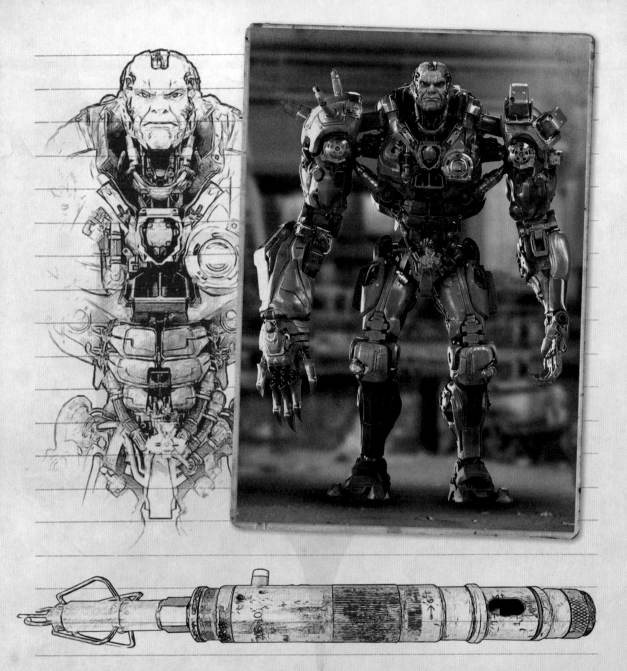

I was staggered when Chiren stepped out from behind Grewishka, proudly taking credit for his upgrades. I can't believe what she's done. Worse, she was after Alita.

Grewishka made it clear that he only wanted Alita and the bar's patrons all made it clear where their loyalties lay — with themselves. Especially as all the Hunter-Warriors knew there was no bounty on Grewishka, so no profit in confronting him. That bastard Zapan would have shoved Alita into Grewishka's hands, but thankfully he was too occupied with holding his broken nose together. Clive Lee summed up the room's mood when he told me I was on my own, but that wasn't quite true.

There was one other courageous soul in the place — a stray dog McTeague had brought into the bar and that Alita had befriended. It leapt between her and Chiren's monster. Grewishka just whipped out his grind-cutter and the segmented blade made short work of the dog.

That got McTeague's full attention, but the Hunter-Warrior still seemed reluctant to interfere.

I tried to appeal to the Hunter-Warriors' heroic side by pointing out that the beast had been killing innocent women — vivisecting them, no less. And when that didn't work, I tried poking at their egos, pointing out how he'd come into their own place of leisure, stolen some of their weapons and was laughing in their faces. "Not our problem."

Through it all, Alita remained composed. I wouldn't have wanted to be her enemy at that moment; the look on her face was terrifyingly calm.

Grewishka and I agreed on one thing: "Iron City is no place for innocence." But I no longer saw an innocent young child when I looked at Alita. And I no longer saw an innocent woman when I looked at Chiren. If Grewishka had ever had innocence, he lost it when he became a disciple of the watcher-behind-the-eyes.

Slowly, deliberately, Alita knelt over the pool of the dog's blood and dipped a finger in the crimson liquid. Then she drew a line in blood across each cheek, under each eye. She raised her eyes to Grewishka and gave him the kind of look you pray you never see as she stood, icy still, and stated, as if reciting a lesson, "I do not stand by in the presence of evil."

And with that, play time was over. Grewishka went into full attack mode. He unleashed the grind-cutter straight at Alita, but she leapt up and twisted in midair as the deadly weapon flew past her. The sound of my hammer's gyros revving up forced Grewishka to turn his sights on me.

You don't realize just how fast grind-cutters are until you have one fired right at you. And perhaps my reflexes aren't what they were in my youth. Thankfully, Hugo tackled me out of the way just as the blades sliced through the air right where my head would have been.

The grind-cutter snaked around the room, slashing apart tables and chairs, and ripping up the floor, all while Alita jumped and flipped out of its path. She paused atop the bar, as if waiting for Grewishka to make another move. Then she leapt at him just as the cutters blasted the bar to pieces… but he knocked her back with a huge fist. She bounced off a column and fell to the ground, momentarily stunned.

Before I could do anything to stop him, Grewishka leapt straight up, then as he dropped, he fired his cutter. Not at Alita, right through the floor and, as his enormous body thundered down, the floor collapsed under the impact.

Grewishka disappeared into a gaping hole, but he wasn't running away. A laugh emerged from deep below us, as he taunted, "Come, little fleaaa…" Half buried in plaster and rubble, I just managed to raise my head in time to see Alita roll to her feet, then unhesitatingly jump into the dark pit.

Hugo and I scrambled down into the Underworld as quickly as we could, using pipes and ladders and whatever else looked sturdy enough to hold us. The sounds of Alita and Grewishka still engaged in their fight to the death floated up to us all the while. Frustrated that I couldn't move as quickly or as recklessly as the cyborgs, I blamed Hugo for inspiring Alita to be such a risk-taker, but his assertion that I'd driven her to this held more truth than I'd like to admit.

We entered into a vast vaulted network of tunnels, a bizarre landscape of giant concrete pillars and rusted pipes. It's the world beneath our world, in the way that Iron City is the world beneath Zalem. It's where Grewishka came from. And where Alita intended to end him.

As I neared the fight, I knew Alita was in trouble. Her cyber blood was leaking from several gashes on her body. She was bleeding heavily from her hip, but it was her knee that concerned me; I could tell she had a malfunctioning leg servo. Without her fast legs, I knew she wouldn't last another second against the hulking beast.

And she didn't. With maniacal determination, Alita leapt at Grewishka once again, but she was forced to dodge midair as he fired his grind-cutters in a wicked blur. Her evasive twist-spin failed and — I can hardly bring myself to write this — the cutters caught her in the air like a scissoring band saw, tearing through her torso, severing one arm, slicing her in half at the waist, and detaching both legs mid-thigh. Alita fell in pieces, her shattered cyber machinery tumbling away from her torn body.

Her shocked expression matched the intensity of the heart wrenching dismay I felt, but our initial reactions were quickly replaced by equal levels of unadulterated rage. As I readied my hammer, running toward them, Alita tried with all her strength to crawl away, dragging her ruined torso by her one remaining arm. Grewishka laughed tauntingly as he knelt down over her. With his huge metal hand, he grabbed her by the hair and jerked her off the ground.

He could have finished her right there and then, squeezed down hard on her head... But he didn't. He threatened to keep her alive instead. Said he'd turn her into a living pendant to adorn his chest, so that he could hear her voice, every moment of the day, pleading for mercy. Of course, if he actually thought she would plead for death, he'd badly misjudged Alita. I have never seen such rage, such a raw will to survive before. The expression looked strangely incongruous on her youthful face.

She drove an open-palm strike into Grewishka's hand, tearing herself out of his grasp. As she fell, she twisted and landed on her hand, perfectly balanced. For a split second, I was amazed by her resilience, but then the harsh reality of the situation snapped back into focus as cyber blood poured out of her gaping wounds and pooled where her cheek touched the ground.

Then she heaved herself upward with extraordinary strength of will, launching straight toward the kneeling cyber-monster's face. She twisted in mid-air to propel herself into a whirling spin. The fingers of her remaining hand formed a blade that skewered deep into Grewishka's eye, twisting in like a corkscrew. She wrenched free by shattering her own wrist joint, and her torn torso crashed to the ground.

It looked like that would be the end of her, as the enraged Grewishka reared back and raised a giant foot to stomp down on her… but I'd finally gotten within striking distance. I triggered my rocket hammer and it blasted into Grewishka's back, tearing open his armor. He roared with rage and knocked my hammer away, but Hugo was ready and threw a fire-bottle that set Grewishka's upper body ablaze. The huge cyborg lunged at us and I truly expected to die right then and there.

Then four flashes of chrome tore past us and hit him hard. It was McTeague's Hellhounds! They ripped into him savagely, their metal jaws tearing apart his armor. Grewishka threw the dogs off and fled into the darkness.

McTeague arrived and called back his well-trained pets, which immediately broke off their instinctive chase of the injured prey. It was obvious that Grewishka's murder of the stray dog had gotten under McTeague's skin, so I barely listened as the Hunter-Warrior explained why he'd belatedly joined the fight. I was too focused on Alita.

I cradled what was left of her shattered form. Her hair was wet with cyber blood and I brushed it out of her eyes. It was my daughter's death all over again. It was almost too much to bear, but I refused to let my grief overwhelm me. Alita needed me.

Hugo grabbed my rocket hammer and we made our way back up into the bar. My heart broke in a whole new way when I saw the look of triumph on Chiren's face. Even though the watcher, Nova, had sent Grewishka to kill Alita, my ex-wife clearly wanted the interloper out of the body we'd built for our daughter.

Chiren thought I was trying to replace our dead daughter... and her... and maybe there was some truth to that. This Alita does ease the pain in my heart. I'm not going to feel guilty about that. I need that. And she needs me, too. I wished Chiren would come back to the Clinic with me, help me save Alita, get to know her for who she is, not as a replacement for our daughter. But I didn't have the time to stop and talk to Chiren. I had to save Alita.

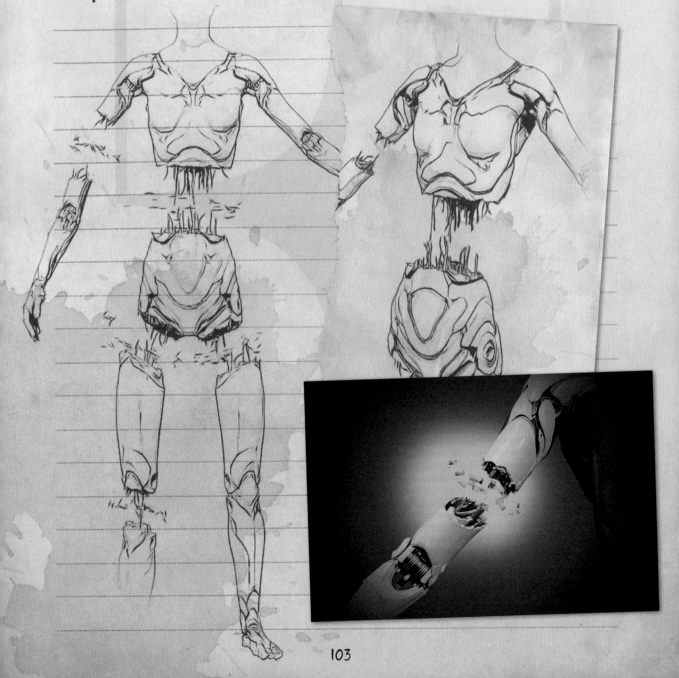

I had to do the very thing I'd sworn I'd never do: Put her core into the Berserker body.

Before I started, I told Hugo I would give him a call when Alita was back on her (new) feet. He left Gerhad and me to our work.

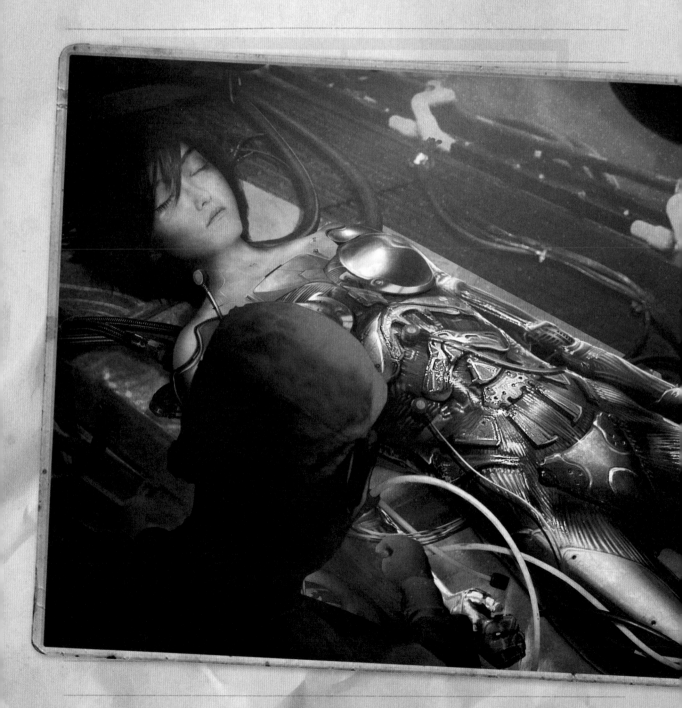

It was a marathon operation, requiring every last drop of cyber blood I had on hand. I'd never worked with a piece of machinery as advanced as the URM Berserker body. Under other circumstances, I could've spent weeks studying the internal systems of the new body.

When I finished, I watched Alita's eyes twitch beneath their lids as she dreamed, bringing on a d j vu of when I'd put her into my daughter's cyber body. Then something amazing happened. Alita's fingers grew a little bit longer. Her waist thinned slightly, her shoulders widened and her chest developed in a way befitting a woman. Nurse Gerhad was enthralled by the transformation. I explained that it was the adaptive technology of the Berserker body — the shell was reconfiguring to Alita's subconscious image of herself. I've never seen anything like it. Micro-adjustments were happening throughout every system.

Alita's cyber core has been married with the body it was intended for. The adult body of a warrior.

We didn't want to leave before she regained consciousness, so Nurse Gerhad and I crashed out in nearby chairs. The next thing I knew, I was being awoken by a gentle kiss on my forehead. I opened my eyes to see my angel. She was a sight to behold. Her new body is sleek and muscular and she was loving it.

Alita bent to the side and balanced on a single fingertip as she lifted her legs straight up in the air, then into a split, then she flipped back onto her feet, all with seemingly no effort, no noticeable strain whatsoever.

I had to admit it. She'd been right. A warrior's spirit needs a warrior's body. And now she has the ultimate warrior's body. She showed me her right hand and I saw tiny blue flames dancing over the tips of her fingers, coming from vents on her arm. Her body was drawing in air then generating an arc plasma, but how it is controlled I couldn't explain to her. The Berserker body didn't exactly come with

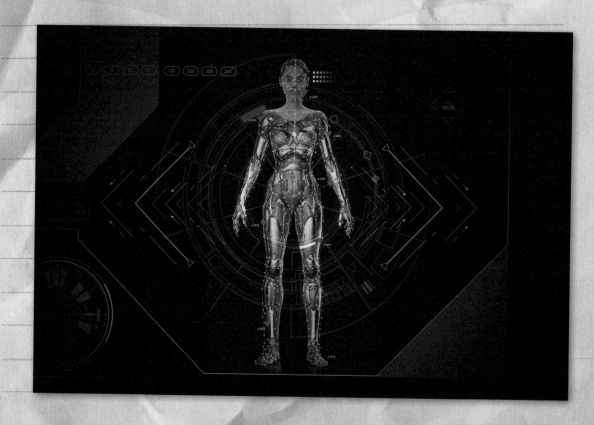

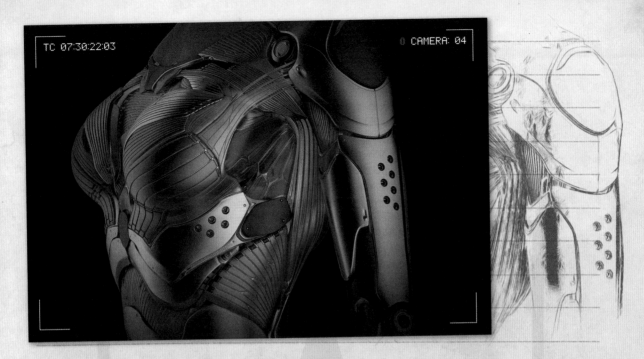

a user's manual. I figured it was safe to assume it was some kind of weapon. One of many, no doubt.

In that body, no one will dare harm her again.

It concerned Alita what side of the war she had been on, but I reassured her that the Berserker body is just a shell. It's not bad or good. What she does with the body is up to her. When she uses it to hug me, that's certainly good. And using it to become a Hunter-Warrior could be good too. She thinks what I do when I take crazed monsters like Grewishka off the streets is noble and I'd like to think she's right.

I've been blaming the games for spawning the dangerous cyber criminals, but Alita argued that the real problem is above. That people like Nova are to blame. She's probably right about that, too, but I don't want her thinking about the world up there. Our world is down here. It's all that matters.

While I knew Alita would be a formidable force for good if she took on the role of Hunter-Warrior, I didn't want her putting her life in danger. So, of course, she chose to try out for Motorball Second League. Not exactly a safe alternative, but it still beats "bagging heads," as she put it.

I hadn't realized how much of a Motorball fangirl Alita had already become until we bumped into Jashugan. We were in the pits as the champ rolled in and his techs swarmed around him. When he saw me, he gave me a warm greeting. I introduced Alita and that's when she started giggling like a star-struck fan. She

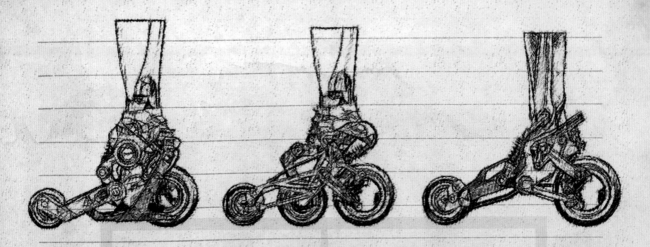

seemed pretty impressed that I know Jashugan.

I was more interested in meeting Ed, Hugo's cyborg mechanic friend. He'd scraped together some loaner gear, giving Alita proper Motorball armor. Not that I'd come emptyhanded myself — I gave Alita a pair of wheel-feet that I'd custom-made for her. They were regulation, but I used all my know-how to make them top-of-the-line and as I made them myself I could guarantee they wouldn't fail her. She did seem touched by my gesture, but was a little preoccupied with her feelings for Hugo. Young love!

She wanted to know if I thought a human could love a cyborg. It seemed like a strange question to me, as I've spent my life making no distinction between the two. And anyway, I wanted her to keep her mind on the game. It gets pretty rough out there, even during tryouts. Truthfully, the thought of my little girl going out on that brutal track was killing me.

I insisted she wear all the pads and the helmet. She insisted she didn't need "all this crap.". I reminded her if she wrecked her new body I couldn't fix it, since it's URM technology. And that was that. She wore the gear. All of it. I wished her luck and made her a deal: I'd stop hovering and making her nervous and she'd go in, race, win, then come right back to me. I should've known it wouldn't be that simple...

Gerhad and I took seats near the pits. I'd expected Hugo to join us to cheer on his "hot pick," but he never showed. I did worry what he'd gotten himself into that would cause him to miss being there for Alita, but I got distracted by the sights and sounds of the track. I hadn't been back there since that day.

Gerhad seemed almost as anxious about me as I was about Alita. I realized that I still love the game, even more than I hate it. But Alita, with "99" scrawled on her shoulder, wasn't playing a game. Only, she didn't know it.

Alita was the sole new tryout, so the game was declared to be "Cutthroat." An irony not lost on me when the other players lined up a moment later. Fortunately, I'd thought to take my flip-down optics with me, to guarantee a clear view.

Alita was supposed to be up against the Factory practice team, but I saw two vicious tattooed punks that had bounty markers on them, right next to some ex-players turned Hunter-Warriors. Though those guys were less HW than mercenaries.

Nothing but a nasty bunch of street iron. For Hunters to be in the same lineup as marks, there could only be one explanation: It was a setup. Someone with serious pull had put this group of thugs together for a very specific reason.

They were there to kill Alita. I called Alita on her internal phone and tried to warn her. I screamed at her to get out of there, but she just wanted to know which of her opponents wanted to kill her. My reply of "All of them!" didn't faze her. If anything, it made her more grimly determined, more laser-focused.

The moment the starting mortar fired the motorball down the track, that monstrosity Stinger swung his giant bladed arms at her head, while Gangsta rushed diagonally at her. Alita reacted as if she didn't notice, like she was just there to race. She exploded off the line and took the lead as the other "players" thundered down the track, giving chase. As furiously as she pumped her legs, the wave of fierce metal behind her started to gain on her. In seconds they were going over 100mph as the unpredictable motorball bounced wildly

down the track, just out of reach. To everyone but me and Gerhad, it looked like an exciting tryout was underway.

Alita dove for the motorball. I held my breath. Stinger was swooping down on her from behind. I could barely watch. But then Alita seized the ball and used it as a mid-air pivot, arcing around and hammering the fifty-pound ball into Stinger's face. He spun backward and slammed into four bunched-up players. The crowd went crazy as bodies ground into the track, metal limbs tearing off in a spray of sparks. A masked thug's fuel line was ruptured, bathing him in burning fuel. The crowd cheered, their attention suddenly riveted on the tryout game.

Most of the players dodged or jumped over the wreckage, and Mace and Kumaza quickly closed in on Alita. Mace swung his mace at her at the same time that the three-wheeled Exploder launched a fireball at her. But everyone underestimated Alita. The URM Berserker body has given her extraordinary stamina and lightning-fast reflexes. Alita ducked just in time. The fireball hit Mace and he veered into Kumaza's path and the two goons went down in a tangled heap. Alita avoided them by leaping onto the barrier wall and skating sideways.

I never completely stopped worrying about her, but I have to admit that for a little while there I watched in breathless awe with the rest of the crowd as Alita took out seemingly non-stop attackers with lightning fast spins, kicks, and blocks. In all the years I'd been involved with Motorball, I'd never seen anything like it.

And neither had anyone else. The practice-game crowd went insane when Alita swung the motorball furiously into the back of a thug's head and knocked it off. They cheered as his bouncing head got kicked out of sight by another player. Then Gangsta gained on Alita, but Stinger sliced him in half before he could attack her. Alita saw Stinger barreling toward her and she spun and hurled the ball at him, taking him out.

No one went after the ball. The remaining thugs dropped all pretense that they were there to play Motorball and focused solely on their mission: To kill Alita.

Alita entered the Traps, weaving through pillars while dodging and blocking blows from blades, maces, and chainsaw arms. In a fusillade of spinning kicks and open-palm strikes, she disabled three opponents in quick succession. Exploder crashed and his turbine exploded. Then Stinger came racing back through the wreckage just as Alita exited the Traps tube. She skated right up a spike obstacle as Stinger swung wildly at her, flipping backwards over him as he impaled himself on the spike.

There was a brief moment when I thought maybe she'd try to escape, but Alita looked back at the tube and waited calmly while, one by one, Screwhead, Mace, Kumaza, and a player I recognised from a Factory "Wanted" poster emerged. They skidded to a stop and formed a ragged line across the track. All of them were damaged and seriously pissed. Stinger most of all, as he freed himself from the spike and glared at Alita.

She taunted them: "Come on! What're you waiting for?"

She seemed to still for a moment, as if listening to an internal voice, and I saw her lips move as she said something. Was she taking a call!? Then she just turned and blasted right through the stadium wall. The drone cameras followed her as she landed in the middle of the street, vehicles swerving around her as she took off through traffic. The players tore through the hole she'd created and raced after her.

I had no idea where she was going, no way of following her. I feared that would be the last time I'd ever see her.

Chiren, of all people, brought her back to me. I didn't dwell on my ex-wife's change of heart. I couldn't. I needed to save Alita's heart — I had to save Hugo's life.

While we were waiting for Hugo to regain consciousness, Alita filled me in on what had happened. Why Hugo had not been at her tryouts and why she'd run off like she had McTeague's Hellhounds on her heels.

Apparently still pissed about being schooled by Alita at the bar, Zapan must have decided to get revenge by killing Hugo. He was crafty, though. As a Hunter-Warrior, he knows better than to straight-up murder a man with no bounty on his head. So he killed a man Hugo and Tanji had just jacked, framing the two of them for murder. Then he went after Hugo, killing Tanji in the process. But Hugo escaped and called Alita for help.

She almost didn't find him in time. Along the way, Screwhead smashed her into a concrete wall. Alita was in no mood for an interruption, so it's a safe bet that Screwhead and the other Factory Motorball thugs didn't know what hit them. Alita says she simply explained to them, "I do not have time for this." But the look in her eyes when she said it tells me they're all scrap now.

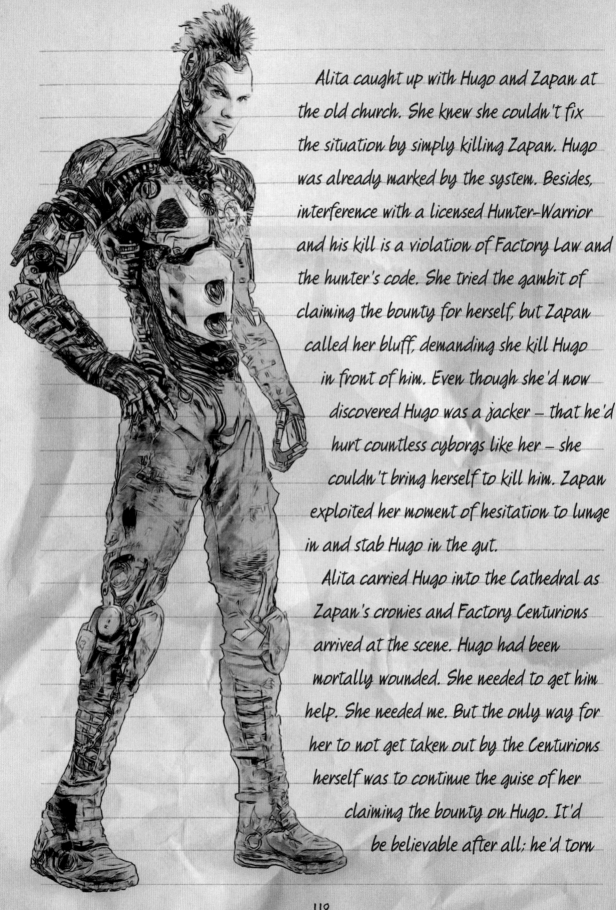

Alita caught up with Hugo and Zapan at the old church. She knew she couldn't fix the situation by simply killing Zapan. Hugo was already marked by the system. Besides, interference with a licensed Hunter-Warrior and his kill is a violation of Factory Law and the hunter's code. She tried the gambit of claiming the bounty for herself, but Zapan called her bluff, demanding she kill Hugo in front of him. Even though she'd now discovered Hugo was a jacker – that he'd hurt countless cyborgs like her – she couldn't bring herself to kill him. Zapan exploited her moment of hesitation to lunge in and stab Hugo in the gut.

Alita carried Hugo into the Cathedral as Zapan's cronies and Factory Centurions arrived at the scene. Hugo had been mortally wounded. She needed to get him help. She needed me. But the only way for her to not get taken out by the Centurions herself was to continue the guise of her claiming the bounty on Hugo. It'd be believable after all; he'd torn

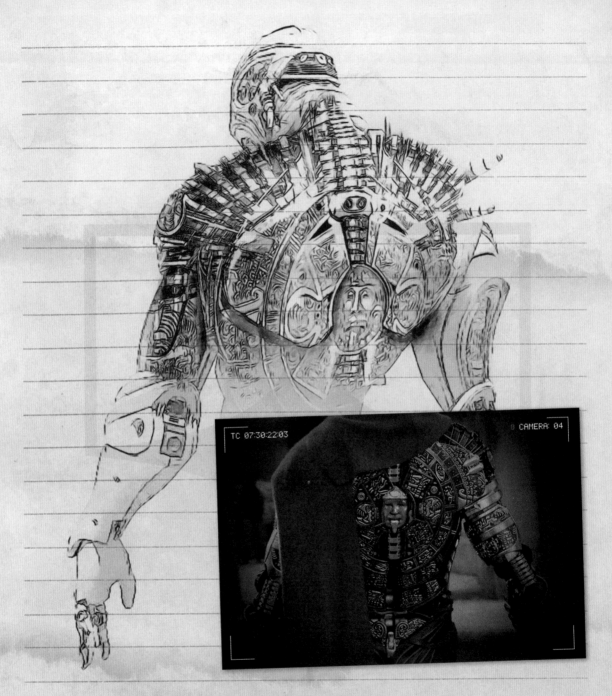

TC 07:30:22:03   0 CAMERA: 04

cyborgs apart for money, so people would assume she hated him.

Alita said Hugo had been jacking to raise the money Vector demanded to get a person up to Zalem. But after he met Alita — _fell in love with her_ — he decided to quit. You could say he'd had a change of heart.

And so had Chiren. She had been spying on Alita and Hugo, yet she told Vector she hadn't found them. Instead, she helped Alita remove Hugo's head and spliced it to Alita's body. They hid the deception with a duffel bag that Alita carried out of the cathedral.

For the sake of the Centurions, Alita was all business: Hunter-Warrior 26651 claiming the kill on bounty 9107.

I wish I could've seen the look of shock on Zapan's handsomely smug face. Alita opened the bag and a Centurion scanned Hugo's head, confirming her claim.

Zapan rushed over to her and yanked at the bag, pulling the canvas away for a better look, and he saw that Alita's chest was open, saw the tubing that pulsed with her blood as her body kept Hugo's brain alive. Alita reacted quickly, concealing what Zapan saw from the others. Desperate, Zapan raised his sword and lunged for Hugo's head.

To the watching Centurions, it looked like Hunter-Warrior F44-269 was attempting to steal another hunter's bounty, which is against Factory Law and the hunter's code. Zapan effectively gave Alita permission to kill him. Instead, she destroyed the thing he loved most: His face. And she did it with his own Damascus Blade. Which she kept. It seems to be an URM weapon, somehow working in concert with the arc plasma produced by the Berserker body.

The URM warrior now has a weapon worthy of her skill.

Hugo is now a Total Replacement cyborg. Chiren's surgical technique at the church was brilliant. There's no brain damage.

Poor Hugo. This city… it corrupts even good people. Vector was scamming him. If you're born on the ground, you stay on the ground. You can't buy your way to Zalem. I told Alita that I should know, as I was born there.

Hugo did not handle the news well. He was raving, unaware of the power of his new body. He nearly destroyed the recovery room before I could administer a sedative. Lucky for him, Alita had already forgiven him. Love is a powerful force.

But she knew they could never be together as long as Nova's lackeys in Iron City were gunning for her. She had no choice but to face the puppets of the watcher-behind-the-eyes. I wanted to go with her, but I knew she would insist I keep watch over Hugo. Perhaps this was her destiny from the day I found her in the Scrapyard.

So I thanked her and let her go. I got to see my little girl grow into an exceptional woman. One who will change the world.

TC 07:30:22:03   0 CAMERA: 04

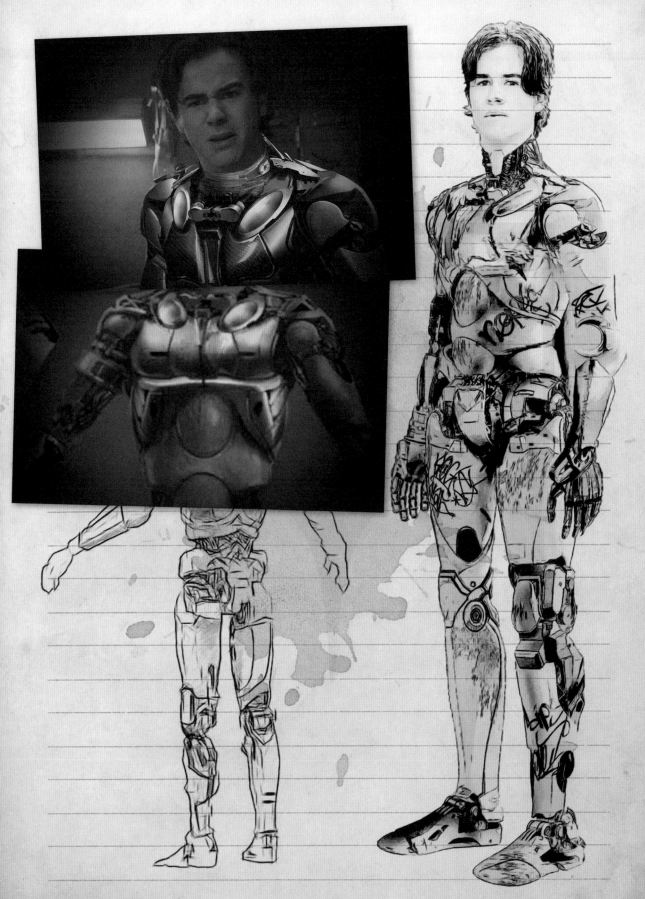

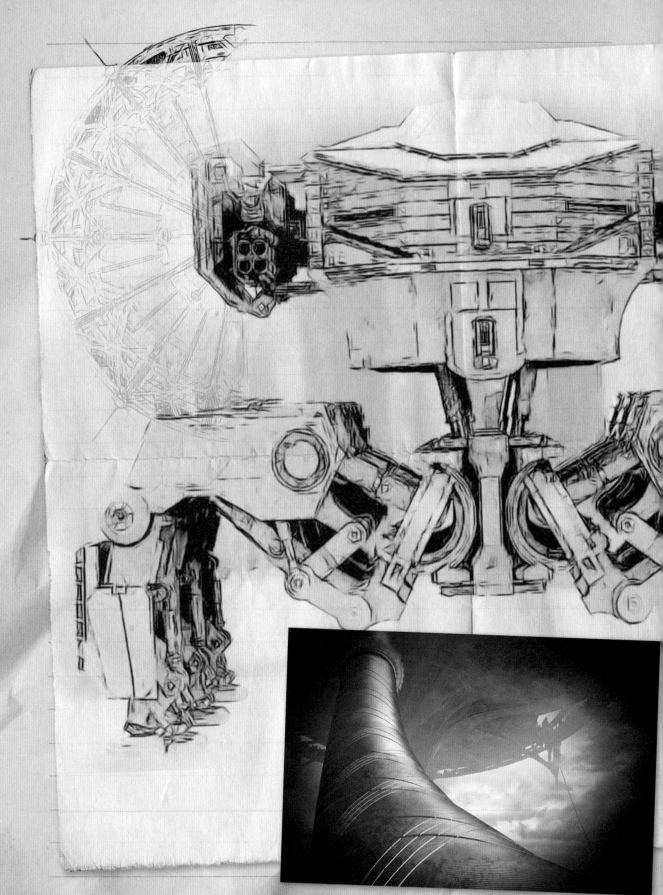

I heard through some other Hunter-Warriors later that Alita tore through the Factory's defensive systems, cutting a swathe through Centurions and Prefects, to get to Vector. Killing him and Nova's champion, Grewishka, with the Damascus Blade.

Unfortunately, she didn't get all of the Factory's numerous enforcers. Some of them came to my Clinic looking for Hugo. I helped him escape, but they sealed the city. They'll find him. He needs Alita's protection. That's why I called her. I think he also needs to know that the person he loves is there for him. Because he's trying to go up by climbing one of the supply tubes that snakes between Iron City and Zalem. And considering the bladed defense rings, that's simply <u>suicidal</u>.

There is only one way to get from the surface to the last sky city, alive. To become Final Champion at Motorball.

If anyone has a shot at that, it's my battle angel, my Alita.

Alita: Battle Angel - Dr. Ido's Journal
ISBN: 9781785658099

Written by Nick Aires.
Nick Aires is a pen-name of Nick Andreychuk. A seasoned fiction and non-fiction writer in the genres of fantasy and horror, Nick is the author of S.T.A.R. Labs: Cisco Ramon's Journal (The Flash), Arrow: Oliver Queen's Dossier, Arrow: Heroes and Villains, and the Official Companions to seasons 1-7 of Supernatural and The Essential Supernatural: On the Road with Sam and Dean (under the pen-name Nicholas Knight). He has also worked as an extra on numerous Vancouver-based TV shows.

Published by
Titan Books
A division of Titan Publishing Group Ltd
144 Southwark St
London
SE1 0UP

www.titanbook.com

First edition: December 2018

10 9 8 7 6 5 4 3 2 1

Did you enjoy this book? We love to hear from our readers. Please e-mail us at: readerfeedback@titanemail.com or write to Reader Feedback at the above address.

To receive advance information, news, competitions, and exclusive offers online, please sign up for the Titan newsletter on our website: www.titanbooks.com

A CIP catalogue record for this title is available from the British Library.

Printed and bound in China.

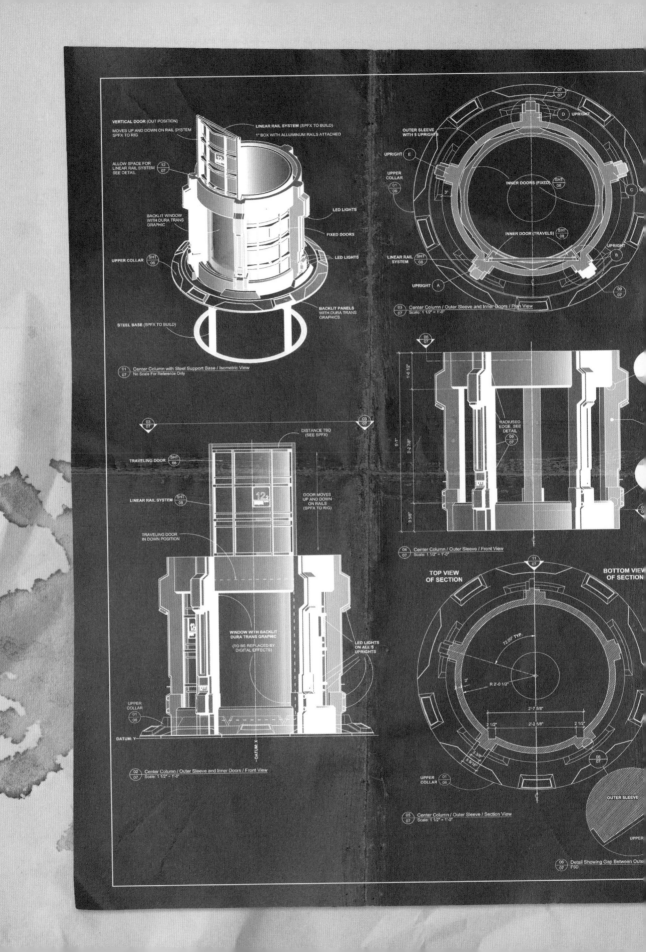

VERTICAL DOOR (OUT POSITION)
MOVES UP AND DOWN ON RAIL SYSTEM
SPFX TO RIG

LINEAR RAIL SYSTEM (SPFX TO BUILD)
1" BOX WITH ALLUMINUM RAILS ATTACHED

ALLOW SPACE FOR
LINEAR RAIL SYSTEM
SEE DETAIL

BACKLIT WINDOW
WITH DURA TRANS
GRAPHIC

LED LIGHTS

FIXED DOORS

LED LIGHTS

UPPER COLLAR

STEEL BASE (SPFX TO BUILD)

BACKLIT PANELS
WITH DURA TRANS
GRAPHICS.

Center Column with Steel Support Base / Isometric View
No Scale For Reference Only

OUTER SLEEVE
WITH 5 UPRIGHTS

UPRIGHT E

UPPER
COLLAR

UPRIGHT D

INNER DOORS (FIXED)

INNER DOOR (TRAVELS)

LINEAR RAIL
SYSTEM

UPRIGHT A

UPRIGHT B

UPRIGHT C

Center Column / Outer Sleeve and Inner Doors / Plan View
Scale: 1 1/2" = 1'-0"

TRAVELING DOOR

LINEAR RAIL SYSTEM

TRAVELING DOOR
IN DOWN POSITION

DISTANCE TBD
(SEE SPFX)

DOOR MOVES
UP AND DOWN
ON RAILS
(SPFX TO RIG)

WINDOW WITH BACKLIT
DURA TRANS GRAPHIC

(TO BE REPLACED BY
DIGITAL EFFECTS)

LED LIGHTS
ON ALL 5
UPRIGHTS

RADIUSED
EDGE. SEE
DETAIL

Center Column / Outer Sleeve / Front View
Scale: 1 1/2" = 1'-0"

UPPER
COLLAR

DATUM: Y

DATUM: X

Center Column / Outer Sleeve and Inner Doors / Front View
Scale: 1 1/2" = 1'-0"

TOP VIEW
OF SECTION

BOTTOM VIEW
OF SECTION

72.00° TYP

R 2'-0 1/2"

2'-7 5/8"

2 1/2"

2'-2 5/8"

2 1/2"

UPPER
COLLAR

OUTER SLEEVE

UPPER

Center Column / Outer Sleeve / Section View
Scale: 1 1/2" = 1'-0"

Detail Showing Gap Between Outer
FSD